S0-DJC-579

T A B L E O F C O N T E N T S

 **ESL VIDEO LIBRARY**

FOCUS ON BUSINESS

KEITH MAURICE

REGENTS/PRENTICE HALL
Englewood Cliffs, New Jersey 07632

Acquisitions Editor: **Nancy Leonhardt**
Production Editor: **Shari Toron**
Prepress Buyer: **Ray Keating**
Manufacturing Buyer: **Lori Bulwin**
Cover Supervisor: **Marianne Frasco**
Cover Design: **Ruta Kysilewskyj**
Cover Photograph: © **1992 Just Blitz/Westlight**
Interior Design: **Tom Nery**
Technical Support: **Molly Pike Riccardi**

ISBN 0-13-007691-0

Prentice-Hall International (UK) Limited, *London*
Prentice-Hall of Australia Pty. Limited, *Sydney*
Prentice-Hall Canada Inc., *Toronto*
Prentice-Hall Hispanoamericana, S.A., *Mexico*
Prentice-Hall of India Private Limited, *New Delhi*
Prentice-Hall of Japan, Inc., *Tokyo*
Simon & Schuster Asia Pte, Ltd., *Singapore*
Editora Prentice-Hall do Brasil, Ltda., *Rio de Janeiro*

ACKNOWLEDGMENTS

This video and text package has been developed with the support and assistance of various people. I would like to thank them publicly here:

Frederick L. Jenks, Professor of Education in the Department of Curriculum and Instruction at Florida State University and Director of the Center for Intensive English Studies at Florida State University. His mentoring, encouragement and support of this project are deeply appreciated.

Alan Waters, University of Lancaster, for what I learned from him about materials writing while we were both in Thailand.

My former colleagues and bosses at the Tokyo Center for Language and Culture, in Japan, (Hisayasu Hosoi, Bernard Johnson, and Eric Hess) and at the Department of Foreign Languages, Mahidol University, (Dhanan Chantrupanth) and at the Sasin Graduate Institute of Business Administration, Chulalongkorn University, (Toemsakdi Krishnamra and Ken Pas) in Thailand, for various opportunities and insights that have led to this project.

Greg Freeman, C.I.E.S., Florida State University, for his thoughtful comments and suggestions on this text.

Nancy Leonhardt, ESL Editor at Prentice Hall Regents, for the opportunity, the various suggestions, and the assistance that went way beyond the call of duty.

Araya Maurice, for special help when it was needed the most.

Finally, I would like to dedicate this text to our two sons, Kevin and Bobby Mac. May your lives be full of love, happiness, health, and success.

INTRODUCTION

The *ABC News ESL Video Library* is a series of interactive, task-based, integrated skills texts for adult learners of English as a second or foreign language. Each text is accompanied by a video, which contains the core presentation of language, and an instructor's manual, which has an answer key and complete transcripts of the videos. This video-based series is unique in that it uses actual broadcast footage from internationally-known *ABC News* programs such as *Business World*, *PrimeTime Live*, *20/20*, *Nightline*, and *World News Tonight* to stimulate students' interest in timely topics presented by world-famous anchors and reporters. More importantly, these broadcast segments provide authentic language input in real situations—nothing has been staged or "set up" artificially. Instead, language instruction flows from the natural language used and is thus always in context.

Each of the texts presents lively topics that are of interest to international students and that relate to life in the U.S. and abroad. Students are encouraged to see U.S. culture in the context of the global village and to bring in their own cultural views to analyze and interpret the video segments.

The instruction utilizes an interactive approach, providing many opportunities for students to work in pairs, small groups, and teams. Students are encouraged to pool their knowledge and learn from one another. In this case, the teacher functions as a facilitator, guiding students through tasks which enable them to discover and learn on their own, rather than as a director.

To make the videos easy to use, time codes have been included in the upper right-hand corner of the screen. These time codes are cross-referenced in the texts so that you can easily find your place on the video. This feature also makes it easier to replay sections you find particularly useful or difficult as many times as you want.

The materials for every segment are divided into five sections: Previewing, Global Viewing, Intensive Viewing, Language Focus, and Post - viewing, all of which lead up to a final task which integrates all language skills. The purpose of each section is as follows:

Previewing challenges students to predict what the segment will cover. This section also helps set the students' schema and enables the teacher to know what information they are bringing with them to class. Occasionally, this section also presents essential vocabulary that the students will need to know in order to understand the segment.

Global Viewing develops students' understanding of the key ideas presented in the segment. In this section, students' overall comprehension and ability to look for main ideas are stressed.

Intensive Viewing zeroes in on specific items for comprehension to prepare students for the final segment task. Students practice looking for details in notetaking and cloze-type exercises.

Language Focus gives practice in the vocabulary and expressions that the students will need to use when completing the final task at the end of the segment.

Postviewing provides a wealth of additional materials, such as charts and readings, all related to the topic of the segment. Students practice analytical and interpretive skills directly related to the final task which appears at the end of this section. The final task integrates language skills and pulls together all of the other language and content skills the students have practiced in the segment.

An additional feature of the videos is that all of the programs, with the exception of *Business World*, are close-captioned. If you have access to a decoder (or if your television has the new decoder chip), you can open up the captions and see the written transcriptions of what the speakers are saying as they speak.

Focus on Business

This text and video contains segments which are all related to the business world. Therefore, all of the final tasks present real situations that are encountered in business, such as debating issues, performing market research and analyses, and developing and critiquing advertising campaigns. The following chart gives you an idea of the scope of this video.

Unit 1: Striving for Success

Segmt.	Function	Final Task
1	• Stating criteria • Discussing and ranking • Evaluating • Deciding • Recommending • Using questions effectively	• Selecting the best company to work for from 3 or 4 different options; OR • Evaluating one company and making recommendations
2	• Stating criteria and reasons • Stating strengths • Suggesting • Stating goals, & objectives • Linking goals to a company • Leading and participating in meetings	• Selecting a successful company; OR • Stating goals & objectives for a company or division
3	• Stating criteria • Preparing & predicting questions • Interviewing roles & strategies • Reporting	• Preparing & conducting interviews

Unit 2: Challenging the Competition

Segmt.	Function	Final Task
4	• Comparing advantages & S.W.O.T. (Strengths, Weaknesses, Opportunities, & Threats) • Analyzing	• S.W.O.T. Analysis
5	• Selecting advantages & reasons • Discussing & deciding • Improving business listening	• Market segmentation and positioning
6	• Comparing benefits & competitors • Analyzing • Interviewing roles & strategies • Reporting	• Market research & analysis

Unit 3: Creating and Selling New Products

Segmt.	Function	Final Task
7	• Predicting • Discussing implications of new trends	• Predicting trends • Discussing implications
8	• Discussing and deciding • Proposing formally • Asking and answering questions • Brainstorming	• New product proposal
9	• Brainstorming • Discussing and deciding • Critiquing/Evaluating • Using formal and informal language	• Creating/doing a commercial • Critiquing a commercial

Unit 4: Globalizing for the Future

Segmt.	Function	Final Task
10	• Discussion strategies for expressing disagreement • Pair debating	• Debating
11	• Rating yourself as a negotiator	• Negotiation (North/South)
12	• Rating cultural tendencies along a continuum • Summarizing negotiation steps	• Negotiating a strategic alliance

Options for Self Study

Although best used in a classroom setting with a teacher facilitating your progress, it is possible to use *Focus on Business* for self study. In this case, you can use the Instructor's Manual to check your answers. When an exercise is interactive and does not have clear-cut answers in the Instructor's Manual, it would be most useful to try to work with a native English speaker who is familiar with the business world to respond to your questions or to work with you. You may also wish to work with a native English speaker for the final task. However, you may simply skip these exercises.

Another useful option for those students who are working alone is to make use of the closed captions. If you have a decoder, you can follow along with the speaker and read the words on the screen. If you do not have a decoder, you can use the transcripts in the Instructor's Manual to reinforce and test your understanding of the videos.

Segment 1

The Best Companies to Work For

from *Business World*, 9/2/90
Runtime: 3:59
Begin: 00:50

Previewing

KEY QUESTIONS

1. What does success mean to you? How do you define it?
2. What are your personal goals and objectives in your business life?
3. What criteria would you use to evaluate companies as places to work?
4. What kind of working situation fits you the best?

DISCUSSION

1. Are there different types of success in life? If so, what are they? If not, explain why not.

   _____

   _____

2. What criteria would you use to decide if you or others are successful?

   _____

   _____

PREDICTION

Based on the title of the segment, *The Best Companies to Work For*, what information do you think will be included in the video segment?

1. _____
2. _____
3. _____
4. _____

ESSENTIAL WORDS TO KNOW

The following words are used in the video segment. Familiarize yourself with the meanings of the words before you view the tape. First, a general definition is given. Then, in the space that follows, write a sentence with the *italicized* word included.

1. *boot camp* = a camp where new military trainees go for training

   _____

2. *criteria* = standards or reasons for choosing something

   _____

3. *make an impact* = have your actions or views be used in the business

   _____

4. *perks* = benefits, other than salary, you get for working; fringe benefits

   _____

5. *guiding premise* = basic belief or assumption

   _____

6. *values* = deeply held beliefs which affect the way you live your life
   and conduct your business

   _____

Global Viewing

GETTING THE GENERAL IDEA

00:50-
02:13

Listen to the first part of the video segment and choose the best answer for each question below:

1. The guiding premise of Tom Peters here is that:
   a. Most companies are bad to work for.
   b. There is no such thing as a great company to work for.
   c. Every company is good for some employees.
   d. The bigger a company is, the better it is to work for.

2. What reason is NOT given for United Parcel Service being a good place to work for?
   a. It is not bureaucratic.
   b. Employees can make a lot of money there.
   c. The company is interested in its employees.
   d. It is especially good for young people with lots of drive.

3. What are three other companies that Tom Peters likes?
   a. MCI, The Body Shop, Pepsico
   b. MCA, Domino's, Pepsico
   c. MCA personal products chain, Domino's, Pepsico
   d. MCI, Pizza Hut, Pepsico

NOTETAKING

The notetaking form below has been partially filled in for you. First read through the notes below so that you know what to listen for. Then, as you view the videotape, fill in the missing information. When you finish, compare your notes with others to check your comprehension. Then watch the video again, filling in any information you missed the first time.

00:50-
04:39

I. Tom Peters' top five companies:

   A. United Parcel Service

   B. MC*I*

   C. The _Body_ _Shop_

   D. _Domino's_ _Pizza_ , delivers for young people with drive

   E. Pepsico, which he calls a great place for managers

II. Three criteria for the best companies, according to Cyrus Friedheim,

   Vice-Chairman of Booz, Allen & Hamilton:

   A. Employees believe "I matter and can make an impact."

   B. There is opportunity to _earn_ and _learn_ .

   C. There's pride in the values of the firm and an identification with its

   mission .

III. Friedheim's unranked choices for best companies:

   A. Amoco

   B. M_c_Donald's

   C Milliken and Company

   D. Motorola

   E. _G_ _E_

IV. Author Lisa Birnbach's four criteria:

    A. first-rate _goods_ and _services_

    B. longevity of relationships

    C. a _merit_ system

    D. thoughtful _perks_

 V. Lisa Birnbach's picks of the best companies:

    A. _3M_

    B. management consultants Bain & Company

    C. _Levi_

    D. _Leo Bernett_ Advertising

    E. _Delta_ Airlines

VI. Northwestern University's Kellogg School of Management Professor Paul Hirsch' criteria:

    A. record for _smart_ management

    B. caring about _employees_

    C. programs for _advancement_

VII. Professor Hirsch's top companies:

    A. Delta Airlines

    B. _Motorola_

    C. _IBM_

    D. Federal _Exp._

    E. Fel-Pro, an auto parts maker

Intensive Viewing

LISTENING FOR DETAILS

Watch the video again, listening for the answers to these questions.

00:50-
04:39

1. Why might some people not enjoy working at UPS?

    Bec. in some ways it is like Marine boot camp.

2. Since General Electric's labor history has not been that good, why does Cyrus Friedheim still think it is a good company to work for ?

    GE has had a vision + focusses on that vision.

3. What does the Delta employee like about working for Delta?

Promotion from within; open-door mgmt. policy

4. Why is Fel-Pro listed with the other, larger companies?

Benefits from recreation to day-care, $2800 coll. scholarship for all employees' children!

CRITERIA & COMPANY COMPARISON

Four people used four different sets of criteria to evaluate companies as places in which to work, and, as a result, came up with different lists of companies. Review your notes, then do the following:

1. CRITERIA: In small groups, organize the criteria listed in your notes into categories so that each criterion is listed next to similar criteria.

Your categories and the number of criteria per category may differ from the chart below.

CATEGORY	CRITERIA
1. _Employee benefits_	a. _Can make you rich (Peters)_
	b. _Can earn + learn (Friedheim)_
	c. _gives thoughtful perks (Birnbach)_
	d. _has progs. for advancement (Hirsch)_
2. _Systems_	a. _Is not bureaucratic (Peters)_
	b. _Has a merit system_
	d. _Believe "I" matter/can have impact (Friedheim)_
3. _Intangibles_	a. _Has Family Atmosphere (UPS employee)_
	b. _Employees have pride/ident. \"/mission (Friedheim)_
	c. _Longevity of relationships (Birnbach)_
4. _Mgmt._	a. _Cares about employees (Hirsch)_
	b. _Has record of smart mgmt. (Hirsch)_
5. _Products_	a. _Produces 1st-rate goods + services (Birnbach)_

2. COMPANIES Which companies are mentioned by two of the evaluators on the video? (1) _Motorola_ and (2) _Delta_ . Use the criteria used in selecting these two companies to get a better picture of the characteristics of each one.

Company: 1. _Motorola_   2. _Delta_

   Criteria: a. _smart mgmt._   a. _smart mgmt._

               b. _Caring_   b. _caring_

               c. _progs. for adv._   c. _progs. for adv._

               d. _"I" matter_   d. _1st rate goods/serv._

               e. _earn & learn_   e. _longevity of relationship_

               f. _pride in Co. values_   f. _merit system_

               g. _____   g. _thoughtful perks_

Compare the two companies as described by the characteristics above. How are they similar and how are they different?

Similarities   Differences

a. _____   a. _____

   _____   _____

b. _____   b. _____

   _____   _____

c. _____   c. _____

   _____   _____

3. Write a one page report about your findings on the criteria and the companies.

Language Focus

CHARACTERISTICS

The following words from the video can be used to describe companies and/or people. Fill in each blank with the appropriate word. Note: (n) = noun, (adj) = adjective.

atmosphere (n)   drive (n)
bureaucratic (adj)   longevity of relationships (n)
vision (n)   mission (n)

1. He is a leader who looks at the big picture and then analyzes the trends in the business world that may influence the direction of the company. He is a man of great _____vision_____ .

2. I like working here because there is a real family ___atmosphere___ .

3. One unfortunate tendency with any organization is that the bigger it gets, the more ___bureaucratic___ it gets.

4. If you aim to own a business of your own, one characteristic you should have is lots of _____drive_____ .

5. In a very competitive environment, where a company's survival is uncertain, and where everyone knows what must be done to help it survive, the company's ___mission___ is quite clear.

6. In large companies in Japan, where lifetime employment is the norm, employees get to know each other very well over a long time. You could say there is a ___longevity of relationships___ .

HARVEST WORDS USED IN BUSINESS

The following words originally came from farming, but are now used in business as well. Listen for these words as you watch the video again. Read the general definition and then write a sentence using the word(s).

1. bear fruit = when one's work results in success

_____

2. the fruits of one's labor = the results of one's work

_____

3. the pickings = the attractiveness of the situation

_____

The following words from the video are used in different ways in business meetings. Read the general definitions and then write a new sentence with each word:

1. accomplish = achieve; do what was expected

   _____

2. fit = match one thing with another; for example, a company fits the
   criteria as a good company in which to work

   _____

3. pick = select; choose _____

4. wrap up = finish; end _____

Postviewing

RELATED READING

Read the following article from *Business Week* to answer the questions that follow:

HOW TO KEEP MANAGERS MOTIVATED

The steady pruning of middle management presents many companies with a problem. Fewer layers mean fewer promotions for promising young managers. A more sluggish economy means less money for raises. So how can companies keep people happy, hard-working, and creative now that the traditional career ladder has lost many of its rungs?

OFFER LATERAL MOVEMENT–It used to be a way to ease managers out. Now it's a way to round them out with fresh challenges. But handle with care: Make it clear that sideways moves aren't a dead end by offering them both to stars and to journeymen.

TURN OVER MORE RESPONSIBILITY–Offer managers more to do--more people to supervise, more areas to influence. Greater control can be more meaningful than a loftier title or even more pay.

TIE RAISES TO PERFORMANCE, NOT SENIORITY–Reduce the number of pay grades to get maximum flexibility in giving raises. That makes it easier to reward people for results, even without an upgrade in title. And broader pay bands pose fewer obstacles to people who want to move across divisions. Don't worry if younger top performers take home more than the seasoned folks who have simply logged the hours.

LET MANAGERS JUST SAY 'NO'–Don't penalize those who turn down transfers or promotions, especially with today's family-cherishing managers. They may feel they're not ready or may want to learn all they can in a current post. Reverse the *Peter Principle*.

OFFER OFFSHORE MOVES–An overseas assignment gives managers a chance to try something new. And their experience will be a plus for increasingly global companies. At Du Pont, for example, where almost half of sales are foreign, a stint overseas is becoming essential for promotion to top management.

PROVIDE MIDCAREER BREAKS–Send promising executives to management development programs at business schools. They can help prepare someone with a specialized background–in science, for example, for general management responsibilities. People will feel rewarded, and the company will get back a more skilled employee.

GIVE MORE POWER–Offer autonomy. Make managers feel like owners–and they'll perform better than if they feel like bureaucrats who have to ask permission at every step. Harness their entrepreneurial impulses before those impulses make them decide to try it on their own.

*Reprinted with permission from *Business Week*, December 10, 1990

EXPERIMENTS IN MOTIVATION

GE Cut the number of pay grades and broadened them dramatically to allow more latitude in raises. Also trimmed management layers from 10 to 4.

HEWLETT-PACKARD Set up a technical track to let scientists advance without taking on management tasks. Now, technicians don't have to manage people to move up.

MERCK Offers variety in career development. For example, scientists can attend law school and become patent attorneys. Encourages movement abroad.

PEPSICO Encourages lateral movement across divisions. Also broadening jobs, so a Taco Bell benefits-plan manager, for instance, can take on recruiting and planning, too.

TRW Offers 'technical fellowships' to engineers, who get generous research budgets and broad latitude to work on projects. Spurs teamwork by sharing Pentagon bonuses.

INTEL Experimenting with job-sharing, putting as many as three managers on teams so fewer people can do more work. Even the chief executive and chairman share jobs.

*Reprinted with permission from *Business Week*, December 10, 1990.

QUESTIONS

1. What has been the direct cause of fewer promotions and raises in many large American companies in the last few years?

   steady pruning of middle mgmt.

2. What new problem has developed as a result of that development?

   How to keep mgrs. motivated

3. What are some alternatives that are being tried at various companies?

   Offer lateral movement; more respon.; tie raises to performance; let mgr. say "no" to transfers; provide mid-career breaks, give more power, etc.

4. Which alternatives, if any, seem particularly worthwhile to you? Why?

5. Which alternatives, if any, seem particularly ineffective or ill-advised to you? Why?

MOTIVATING MANAGERS

In *How to Keep Managers Motivated*, seven suggestions were offered, while *Experiments in Motivations* listed the specific solutions being tried at various companies. Which companies are using motivational techniques laid out in *How to Keep Managers Motivated*? Write the letter(s) of the techniques next to the name of the company.

1. GE _C_
2. Hewlett-Packard _N/A_
3. Merck _e, f_
4. Pepsico _a, b_
5. TRW _b_
6. Intel _N/A_

a. Offer lateral movement
b. Turn over more responsibility
c. Tie raise to performance, not seniority
d. Let managers just say "no"
e. Offer offshore moves
f. Provide midcareer breaks
g. Give more power

PREPARATION FOR THE MEETING

Knowing how to use questions effectively to move meetings along is an important business communication skill. The quiz below indicates some common concerns that many meeting leaders and participants have.

EFFECTIVE USE OF QUESTIONS

Select a response from the right-hand column which correctly describes what you would do in the situations described in the left-hand column. Write the letter corresponding to your choice on the line in front of the number of the situation. (It is all right to repeat a response.)

Situation	Response
_c_ 1. You want to stimulate discussion.	(a) Ask each participant to summarize the other's position.
_h_ 2. You want to cut off discussion.	(b) Ask for feedback from the group.
_f_ 3. You want to bring a participant into the discussion.	(c) Ask the group a general question.
_d_ 4. Two participants are engaging in side conversation.	(d) Ask an individual a specific question.
_i_ 5. You are asked a question you are not sure you can answer.	(e) Ask the group a specific question.
_e_ 6. You want to test the level of support for a point of view.	(f) Ask an individual a general question.
_h_ 7. Two participants are debating a point. Everyone else is watching.	(g) Ask the group for a summary.
_g_ 8. Discussion has been going on for some time. You're unclear of progress.	(h) Ask an individual to summarize the discussion.
_a_ 9. Two people have been debating a point without much progress.	(i) Direct the question back to the group.
_b_ 10. You would like to know if you have been an effective leader.	(j) None of the above.

Reprinted by permission of Crisp Publications Inc. from *Effective Meeting Skills* by Marion Haynes, pp. 52-53 and 94.

FINAL TEAM TASK: DECISION-MAKING MEETINGS

Choose one of the following tasks to do as a team:

1. a. Decide on the your own set of criteria to evaluate companies as places in which to work.
   b. Get as much relevant information as you can about 3-4 companies from library reference books, company materials, interviews, and other sources of information.
   c. Discuss and rank the companies based on your criteria.
   d. Give a formal presentation on your decisions on criteria and companies.
2. a. Decide on your own very specific and detailed list of criteria to evaluate one company as place to work.
   b. Evaluate the company based on your criteria.
   c. Discuss and list alternatives that the company could follow to make it a better place in which to work.
   d. Decide on recommendations that you would like the company's leaders to implement in order to make the company a better place in which to work.
   e. Give a formal presentation to the company's leaders, focusing on your criteria, the company's performance based on the criteria, possible alternatives, and your recommendations.

FINAL TASK

Write a concise, yet thorough report on your personal goals and objectives in business (and personal life if you so desire) for this year, the next five years, the next ten years, and beyond.

Segment 2

Wal-Mart: What is the Secret of its Success?

from *Business World*, 4/21/91
Runtime: 4:20
Begin: 04:50

Previewing

KEY QUESTIONS

1. Can you plan for business success? If so, how do you do so?
2. What strategies can help retail businesses succeed?
3. What strategies can help other types of businesses succeed?
4. What criteria can you use to assess the success of companies? Which are the key criteria?

DISCUSSION

1. Can you plan for business success? If so, how do you do so? If not, why can't you do so? _____

_____

2. What strategies can help retail businesses succeed?

_____

_____

PREDICTION

Based on the title of the segment, *Wal-Mart: What is the Secret of its Success?*, and your own background knowledge, what information do you think will be included in the video segment?

1. _____

2. _____

3. _____

The following words and expressions are used in this video segment. Match each word to its definition.

1. be on the leading edge _b_
2. chain _f_
3. have a knack for _d_
4. homespun _a_
5. magnate _e_
6. responsive _c_

a. plain and simple
b. be the first or best
c. sensitive, sympathetic
d. have the talent to do something well
e. great business leader
f. group of stores

Global Viewing

SOUND OFF

05:07-
06:46

With the sound turned off, watch the first part of the video and then answer the following questions:

1. What kind of person do you think Sam Walton is? _____
   old-fashioned, unpretentious

2. Where (or at what kind of place) is Wal-Mart's headquarters located? ___
   In small city, not in a skyscraper in NY

3. What is one specific reason for Wal-Mart's success?_____
   technology

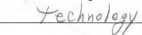

NOTETAKING

05:07-
09:10

The notetaking form below has been partially filled in for you. The form is organized by theme, not by sequence. First read through the notes, then view the video tape, filling in the missing information. When you finish, compare your notes with others to check your comprehension.

I. Company History

    A. Began in (year) _1945_

    B. 1974:

        1. New equipment used _(scanners) computers_

        2. Cost of 1000 shares of stock = $ _1650_

C. "Last year":

   1. Sales: _____ *32.6 b* _____

   2. Number of new stores: _____ *143* _____

   3. Sales revenue % increase in one year: *26* %

D. "This year":

   1. Cost of 100 shares of stock = $ *2 mil.*

II. Characteristics and Special Features of Wal–Mart

   A. (is) responsive to *Shareholders*

   B. (is) responsive to *Customers*

   C. (has) a knack for *expanding in diff. times*

   D. (has) distribution centers that *deliver goods to its stores* *(most others (4-8 days))*
   in about 30 hrs.

   instead of four to eight days.

   E. (has) *Computer* links to manufacturers.

   F. (has) "people *greeters* " *to welcome* customers, a
   Buy *American* program to *encourage US prod.*, and
   ongoing *experiments.*

III. The Real Key to Success: *giving cust. what they want*

_____

IV. Characteristics and Feelings of its Workforce

   A. a fine *work ethic*

   B. *integrity*

   C. *honesty*

   D. not employees, but rather *assoc. who work hards*

   E. share *profits*

   F. feel *part of a team*

V. One Experiment You Probably Won't See in New York, Chicago, or Los
   Angeles: *Worm bar*

_____

Intensive Viewing

(**LISTENING CLOZE**)

The passage below is the first part of the video. Watch this section again and fill in the blanks with the missing words:

Sander Vanocur: It may not be easy being number one, but it can be _____fun_____. Wal-Mart, now the nation's number-one _retailer_, has also been rated number one in _responsiveness_ to its shareholders by the United Shareholders Association. But that's not a surprise for a _chain_ that built itself up to number one by being _responsiveness_ to its customers.

Tucked away in the tranquility of the Ozarks is a Bentonville, Arkansas, five-and-dime that's now a monument to America's most successful retailing _magnate_.

Sam Walton: It's hard to realize that we've come from that one store, and it wasn't all that many years ago – like, what, _46_ years now?–to where we are today. But it's just been one store at a time, maybe two or three.

Sander Vanocur: Last year, it was _143_, at a time when many retailers _downsized_. And Wal-Mart's sales revenue soared _26_ percent, to a mindboggling $ _32.6_ billion, knocking out Sears as the nation's largest retailer. Wal-Mart has a _knack_ for expanding in difficult times — in Texas during the oil _bust_ ; in the troubled Northeast now.

Language Focus

The words and expressions below are often used in business situations. Watch the video again, listening for the words below. Try to guess the meaning of the words from the way they are used by the speakers. Write your own definition.

05:07-
09:10

1. access: _____ *get connected to* _____

2. adopt: _____ *begin to use* _____

3. downsize: _____ *reduce* _____

4. knock out: _____ *move ahead of competition* _____

5. link to: _____ *access connected to* _____

6. soar: _____ *increase by a large margin* _____

Now read the sentences below. Then use the italicized word in a sentence of your own.

1. If a manufacturer is computerized, it may be able to *access* the store computer to see how its products are selling. _____

_____

2. Sometimes it is essential for companies to quickly *adopt* new technology while at other times it may be wise to wait a while before using it. _____

_____

3. While some companies are expected to expand significantly in the 90's, others are going through painful *downsizing.* _____

_____

4. We have to be responsive to our customers and meet their needs in order to *knock out* our major competitors. _____

_____

5. If a retailer *links to* a manufacturer by computer, it can find out whether merchandise has been shipped. _____

_____

6. It was a great year for us. Sales *soared* 30% over last year, and our market share is increasing. _____

_____

Postviewing

RELATED READING: RANKING COMPANIES

Read the following chart and then rank the companies according to the criteria below:

STATE OF THE INDUSTRY				
(from *Chain Store Age Executive*, August 1991, excerpts from p. 5a)				
Company	1990 Revenues (billion)	1989 Revenues (billion)	1990 Profits (million)	1989 Profits (million)	Stores 1990 *1989*
1. Wal-Mart	$32.6	$25.8	$1,291	$1,076	1721 *1525*
2. Kmart	$32.1	$29.5	$ 756	$ 323	4180 *4259*
3. Sears	$32.0	$31.6	$ 257	$ 647	1765 *1731*

Rankings:

	Wal-Mart	Kmart	Sears
1. 1990 Revenues:	1	2	3
2. 1989 Revenues:	3	2	1
3. 1990 Profits:	1	2	3
4. 1989 Profits:	1	3	2
5. Number of Stores (1990):	3	1	2

RELATED READING: COMPARING COMPANIES

Read the article below and then fill in the grid that follows:

THE DISCOUNT DEPARTMENT STORE INDUSTRY: THE NEW "BIG 3"

Sears, J.C. Penney and Montgomery Ward have given way to Wal-Mart, Kmart and Target as the new retailing "Big 3" of mass market retailing. Merger and acquisition activity, company failures, bankruptcies and industry consolidation have resulted in an industry dominated by fewer, but larger and more powerful players. The top 10 discount department store retailers now represent 85.3% of industry sales, with Wal-Mart, Kmart and Target alone accounting for nearly three-fourths of total industry volume. Each of the "Big 3" have unique strengths and distinctive market positions:

•In 1990, Wal-Mart overtook Kmart as the largest discounter. The company grew rapidly during the last five years, expanding its traditional base of smaller-sized, secondary market stores, branching out into membership warehouse and supercenter formats, and developing an upsized discount store prototype for larger population centers and markets with higher expenditure potential.

Key advantage: Currently, Wal-Mart possesses the low cost advantage over both Kmart and Target, and is clearly in a position to continue leveraging this advantage.

Challenges: For long-term competitive viability, however, an effort equal to the investment in systems will be required in terms of store decor and the shopping environment. Additionally, Wal-Mart's ability to compete in highly competitive markets, and its ability to meet the volume requirements of those areas, is still unproven.

•Target is progressing well in the development of systems support and is poised for rapid growth through store expansion.

Key advantage: Target has successfully established itself as the leading "upscale" discount department store.

Challenges: As Target continues to move upscale, the key question will be whether there is enough demand to support an upscale discount department store operation as it begins to bump up against highly promotional and lower end department stores.

•While Kmart has achieved only very slow growth in its core conventional, full-time discount store business, it has concentrated growth efforts on diversification into various specialty mass market concepts. Remodel and upgrading efforts for the past several years are positive.

Key advantage: Kmart's exceptional network of metro locations.

Challenges: Kmart is caught in the middle, with neither the low cost advantage of Wal-Mart, nor the upscale presence of Target. While its locations are good, site selection is somewhat constrained by Kmart's larger store size. Additionally, the company continues to work through challenging organizational and system support requirements.

SUMMARY GRID

	Wal–Mart	Target	Kmart	Smaller stores
General developments	Overtook K-Mart as #1 discounter, growing rapidly in last 5 yrs.	Progressing well in systems support, poised for growth	Low growth, but diversifying in specialties & remodeling efforts	diff. to compete re: vendor relocation + allocating resources
Key advantage	low cost	leading "upscale" discounter	network of metro locations	none
Challenges	store decor, shopping environment; highly competitive environment	enough demand for "upscale" discounter?	caught in middle, site selection probs, organizational probs.	technology, refurbishing + competitive serv, + inventories

INTERPRETING THE READING

After reading the article, put Wal–Mart, Kmart and Target in the appropriate spots in the matrix below.

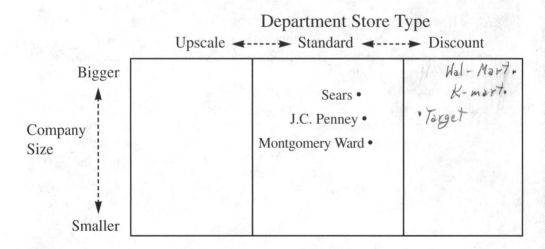

GENERAL MEETING SKILLS

Successful business meetings depend in large part on the skillful leadership and participation of everyone involved. Take a few minutes to rate yourself as both a meeting leader and participant. Then compare your self-evaluation with others. This will be useful to you for the final task and for many meetings to come.

1. How well do you lead business meetings?

Answer the following questions honestly. (EX= excellent / GO= good / AV= average / FA= fair / PO= poor)

Skill	EX	GO	AV	FA	PO
1. Set clear objectives					
2. Prepare agenda & give to people before meeting					
3. Appoint someone to keep notes & write up minutes					
4. State purpose clearly					
5. Review agenda at meeting and revise if necessary					
6. Follow the agenda					
7. Encourage participation					
8. Encourage & support disagreement					
9. Listen well					
10. Handle difficulties effectively, e.g., conflicts, passivity, etc.					
11. Keep discussions on task					
12. Clarify statements and misunderstandings					
13. Summarize decisions					
14. Follow up after meeting					
15. Other _____					

2. How well do you participate in business meetings?

Skill	EX	GO	AV	FA	PO
1. Know purpose of meeting					
2. Prepare for the meeting					
3. Listen well					
4. Respect views of others					
5. Speak clearly & concisely					
6. Stay focused on agenda					
7. Give ideas in positive way					
8. Cooperate to achieve objectives of meeting					
9. Follow up after meeting as needed					
10. Other: _____					

FINAL TEAM TASK: DECISION-MAKING MEETINGS

Choose one of the tasks below to do as a team. First select a leader; then, as you have the meeting, remain aware of the checklists above.

TASK #1

1. Decide on key criteria for selecting successful companies.
2. Select a company that fits your criteria.
3. Discuss why it has become and is successful. Decide on the top 3-5 strategies for the company's success and how each has contributed to the success. You may use the following factors to guide discussion:

    a. Top leadership vision
    b. Management skills
    c. Employee skills
    d. Management-labor relations
    e. Relations with suppliers
    f. Customer service
    g. Product development
    h. Luck

    i. Product quality
    j. Product cost
    k. Use of technology
    l. Manufacturing skills/operations
    m. Capital/finance
    n. Marketing skills
    o. Government policy
    p. Other _____

4. Select one spokesperson to report on the content of the team's decisions. Select another spokesperson to report on the process of the team's decision-making, using the checklists above to describe the strengths of the meeting and how the meeting could have been improved.
5. Have the representatives give their formal reports.

TASK #2

1. Pick a company, division, or department in a company.
2. Decide what its general goals, specific objectives, strategies and tactics should be for the next year, next five years, and next 10 years. In so doing, be sure to:

   a. Link the tactics, strategies, objectives to the goals.
   b. Explain why the goals, objectives, strategies and tactics fit the organization.

3. Select one spokesperson to report on the content of the team's decisions. Select another spokesperson to report on the process of the team's decision-making, using the checklists above to describe the strengths of the meeting and how the meeting could have been improved.
4. Have the representatives give their formal reports.

EXECUTIVE SUMMARIES

Write a clear and concise summary of either task #1 or task #2 above. Include in your summary the key information on both the content and process tasks.

Segment 3

An International Success Story: Akio Morita

from *Nightline,* 4/24/90
(edited)
Runtime: 13:46
Begin: 09:32

Previewing

KEY QUESTIONS

1. What are the key personal skills and characteristics needed to achieve success in business? Which skills and characteristics are especially needed internationally?
2. What are useful business strategies to enhance one's (or one's company's) success?
3. What are some useful personal strategies that can help or enhance one's (or one's company's) success?
4. Can those skills, characteristics, and strategies be developed through training programs? If so, how? If not, why not?
5. How can you perceive whether someone has the necessary skills and characteristics to help a company become more successful?

PREDICTION

The first video segment is a profile of Akio Morita, founder of the SONY Corporation. Based on your background knowledge of Mr. Morita and SONY, what information do you think will be included on the video?

1. _____
2. _____
3. _____

ESSENTIAL WORDS TO KNOW

The following words will be used in the video. Read the words as they are used in the following sentences and try to come up with your own definition.

1. Companies are sometimes viewed as *commodities* themselves and are bought and sold in the U.S.

    commodity: _Something th.is bought or sold_

2. He *is very critical* of some of the business practices of his company; he thinks they are not doing what's best for the employees.

    (*be very*) *critical*: _find fault with_

3. She is an *entrepreneur* who has built her own company from the ground up.

    entrepreneur: _a business person who starts + builds a business_

4. In New York, *Madison Avenue* firms are among the top advertising agencies in the world.

    Madison Avenue: _a St. in NYC where many ad. firms are found_

5. They think the President's trip to Japan was just a *ploy* to get more votes at home rather than to try to come to an agreement with Japanese businesses.

    ploy: _an act, strategy, or maneuver_

6. The new sales manager disagrees with the policies of her *predecessor* and is trying to make many changes.

    predecessor: _a person who came before_

Global Viewing

COMPREHENSION CHECK

View the video from the beginning up to, but not including the interview. As you watch, check the appropriate answers to the following questions.

09:32-
14:52

	True	False	Not Sure	Not Given
1. The Japanese-American economic relationship is a very simple one.		✓		
2. Americans resent Japanese salesmanship.	✓			
3. SONY's sales last year exceeded $16 billion.	✓			
4. Akio Morita's first business was running the family saki brewery.		✓		
5. Mr. Morita's $500 stake to begin SONY came from his friends.		✓		
6. President DeGaulle of France was very impressed by Mr. Morita		✓		
7. SONY bought the rights to manufacture the transistor from Western Electric in 1952.	✓			
8. SONY had problems at first in selling its pocket radio.	✓			
9. Mr. Morita knew early on the value of selling internationally.	✓			
10. SONY is bigger in the U.S. than it is in Japan.	✓			
11. Mr. Morita's style is typical of established Japanese businessmen.		✓		
12. When Mr. Morita co-authored a book critical of the U.S., he wanted Americans to read it.		✓		

Intensive Viewing

VIEWING CLOZE

09:32-11:27

The passage below is the first part of the video transcript. View the first part of the video and fill in the blanks with the missing words.

Ted Koppel: His name is Akio Morita. He's the chairman of the board of the SONY Corporation, one of the _world's_ most successful companies. Mr. Morita is highly _critical_ of the way Americans do _business_. Among his charges, that if we've _lost_ our competitive edge, we have only ourselves to blame. We'll see what we can learn from him tonight

Announcer: This is ABC News Nightline. Reporting from _Washington_, Ted Koppel.

Ted Koppel: It's something along the lines of a _love_ - _hate_ relationship. We admire Japanese salesmanship and _products_ even as we resent the inroads that _both_ are making here in the United States. We are _convinced_ that somehow Japan is using a double _standard_, flooding the market with its products while _making_ the sale of U.S. goods in Japan next to _impossible_.

And while that is at least _partially_ true, we pay less attention to the _fact_ that the Japanese businessmen who come to this _country_ speak English and have taken the _trouble_ to learn something about our customs, while it is the _rare_ American businessman who takes that kind of _knowledge_ of Japanese language and customs with him to Japan.

We are _hurt_ when one of the most successful Japanese businessmen of our _generation_, the founder and chairman of SONY, accuses Americans, _in_ _effect_, of being a nation of cry babies. Well, maybe Akio Morita's very _success_ has earned him our attention. Here's a short _profile_ by Nightline correspondent Jackie Judd.

INTERVIEW NOTETAKING

In his interview with Ted Koppel, Mr. Morita contrasts typical Japanese business operations with typical American business operations. View the video filling in the notetaking grid below with the main points he discusses. When you finish, compare your notes with others to check your comprehension.

Points covered:	Japanese Mgmt.	American Mgmt.
1. Attitude toward company	for group	for elite mgmt,
2. New manager's style	(not given)	show his ability
3. Profit orientation	long-term	short-term (yrly)
4. Ways to make money	invest in future	move money
5. Way of treating company	like a group	like a commodity
6. Way of viewing employees	as a family	like commodities
7. Hiring/laying off policies	do not lay off easily	hire + lay off easily

NOTETAKING

View the next part of the video, a report on how American corporations treat their workers, and fill in the notetaking form below. Compare your notes with others to check your comprehension.

1. a. Joanne Sullivan's past efforts: worked for Co. 25 yrs.

   b. feelings: sad

   c. desire: to work, Not be on welfare

2. American business/economy in last decade:

   a. economic restructuring: biggest in history

   b. corporate profits: ↑ by 70%

   c. workers laid off (#): 10,000,000

   d. worker morale: plummeted (went down quickly)

   e. trust in management: "declined"

   f. belief in managerial competence: less than before

   g. belief in managerial respect for workers: less than before

   h. top-level managerial incomes: 50-500x av. worker compared

      to top level Japanese incomes: 10x more than workers

3. James Fallows' views:
   a. Best place to be at the top: _USA_
   b. Best place to be at the bottom: _Japan_
4. Policies of large Japanese companies:
   a. On job security: _lifetime_
   b. On decision-making: _workers are part of it_
   c. On conformity: _workers are expected to conform_
   d. On overall style: _paternalistic_
   e. On living arrangements: _liv. in Co. dorms_
   f. On finding a wife/husband: _boss to help find_
   g. On vacations: _scarce_
   h. On workdays: _12 hr. days_
5. What Japanese can learn from Americans: _enjoy life more_
6. What Americans can learn from Japanese: _worker involvement, cont. improvement, att. to detail._

Language Focus

VOCABULARY CHECK

Read the short passages below. View the first part of the video again, listening for the following sentences. After each passage, select the best synonym for the *italicized* word.

1. He is *critical* of the way they do business. Among his many *charges*, perhaps the most important is that they have lost their *competitive edge*.
   1. *critical*:
      a. is neutral about   b. is enthusiastic about
      c. is supportive of   d. is unhappy about
   2. *charges*:
      a. demands   b. accusations
      c. suggestions   d. views
   3. *competitive edge*:
      a. ability to compete   b. key business customers
      c. cost advantage   d. quality advantage

2. We admire their salesmanship and products even as we resent the *inroads* that both are making here. We are *convinced* that somehow they are using a *double standard*, flooding our market with their products while making the sale of our goods there next to impossible.

   1. *inroads*:
      a. market penetration   b. market damage
      c. progress   d. drive

   2. *convinced*:
      a. skeptical   b. sure
      c. nervous   d. unhappy

   3. *double standard*:
      a. an improved quality   b. the top quality
      c. a fine accomplishment   d. unfair practice

3. He *presides over* a company with sales last year *exceeding* the gross national product of many countries. He began the company with a small *stake* from his family.

   1. *presides over*:
      a. supervises   b. worries about
      c. competes with   d. is pursuing

   2. *exceeding*:
      a. more than   b. as much as
      c. almost as much as   d. approaching

   3. *stake*:
      a. emblem   b. amount of funds
      c. group of supporters   d. idea for a company

4. He bought *the rights* to manufacture the product in his country. After a creative solution to an initial problem, the company was *off and running*. It then hired a *Madison Avenue* firm to help it succeed in the U.S.

   1. *the rights*:
      a. the permission   b. the blueprints
      c. the company   d. the subsidiary

   2. *(be) off and running*:
      a. struggling to survive   b. growing smoothly
      c. surviving, but struggling   d. exercising

   3. *Madison Avenue*:
      a. advertising   b. financial
      c. accounting   d. legal

5. Is he a member of the *old-line* business *elite* or is he more of a
   buccaneer entrepreneur?
   1. *old-line*:
      a. low tech   (b.) well established
      c. past   d. liberal
   2. *elite*:
      (a.) powerful group   b. fashionable group
   3. *buccaneer entrepreneur*:
      (a.) adventurous businessperson   b. reckless employee
      c. unstable businessperson   d. beginning employee

Postviewing

X **COMPARING COMPANY POLICIES**

The video segments have looked at policies of large Japanese and American
companies that are typical in Japan and the U.S. The policies do not
describe every company in each nation. With that in mind, discuss one or
both of the following questions with others. First, designate a meeting
leader and a representative to report your team's conclusions to the class.

1. How do the policies of typical large Japanese companies compare with
   those of large companies in other nations? (Either those in your nation
   or those in other nations you are familiar with.) Would it be advisable
   and feasible to make policies more like those of the large Japanese
   companies? Why or why not?
2. Choose one company and compare its policies with those of a typical
   large Japanese company? Would it be advisable and feasible to make the
   policies more like those of the large Japanese companies? Why or why
   not?

X **RELATED READING: ARE YOU INTERNATIONABLE?**

Read the following excerpts from *Going International: How to Make Friends
and Deal Effectively in the Global Marketplace* by Lennie Copeland and Lewis
Griggs. Then answer the questions that follow. The excerpts are from
Chapter 12: *The Road to Success: What does it take to be a winner?*

The Road to Success: What does it take to be a winner?

"At the risk of stating the obvious," says Frank De Angeli, Johnson & Johnson's senior international executive, " the essential ingredient in conducting international business is people . . . having the right people in international assignments." Some people are just not cut out for international work, and some are effective and happy in some cultures but not in others. Before making or accepting an overseas assignment, careful selection and honest self-selection is a process warranting serious attention.

Are you internationable?

What are the characteristics of people who are successful overseas? When we analyze everything we have learned from international travelers, expatriates, heads of personnel, foreigners and diplomats, we can boil down to one word the difference between people who do especially well abroad and those who do not: breadth. The person who does well abroad must know not only the job and company, as he or she does at home, but also the cultural patterns, business norms, and national character of the assigned country. This knowledge must be founded on an understanding of the country's history, arts, politics, economic conditions, and so on. Those who succeed show breadth of knowledge and intellectual curiosity, but also breadth of character—an open-arms and open eyes personality. They are what one expert calls "geocentric" in attitude, thinking in world terms and seeing opportunities, not constraints, in the millions of differences they encounter abroad. Looking closely at the personalities, attitudes and skills of people who perform at high levels of excellence abroad, we have settled on seven success traits that seem to define the person of "breadth," and which make the difference, wherever the assignment and whatever the job. Of course, in certain countries individuals will need qualities peculiarly adapted to the demands of the particular environments, and careful attention should be paid to those unique demands.

Success trait 1: Hard like water

Claus Halle, president of Coca-Cola's international soft-drink business sector, says: "The key to developing our international business lies not in the rigid application of a global strategy, but in a flexible planning system, heavily reliant on input from the market and able to respond quickly to shifts in local growth and competitive conditions." Hans Becherer, senior vice president of Deere & Company's Overseas Division, says much the same: in a word, the key to international success is "flexibility." A company needs all the attributes and qualities that make it successful in its home market," Becherer says. "In addition, it must take into account differences in culture and marketplace, as well as international realities such as shifting currencies and political relationships." The international individual, like the international company, needs to be adaptable to succeed abroad. Words such as "flexible" and "adaptable" should not suggest an individual who is weak, malleable, compliant, a pushover. Our successful people abroad are not pushovers. They do not bend to every wind, nor adapt like chameleons to each circumstance—quite the contrary. But neither are they rigid, immovable or unimpressionable. They are what the Japanese would call "hard like water." Water goes with the flow, bending with the turns in the riverbed, but its water that carved out the Grand Canyon. Water is soft and takes the shape of its container, but water can carry the load of a thousand-ton ship. The internationable person and water have another trait in common: if you watch the river, you will see that it is always the same while it is always changing. (pp. 209-210).

Summary

The internationable person is characterized in a word: *breadth.*

Success Traits that Define the Internationable Person

1. Hard like water.
2. Resourceful independence through people.
3. Curiosity.
4. Positive regard for others.
5. Emotional stability.
6. Technical competence.
7. Motivation.

Reprinted with permission from *Going International: How to Make Friends and Deal Effectively in the Global Marketplace,* by Lennie Copeland and Lewis Griggs, 1985, McGraw-Hill, pp.209-210 & 218.

QUESTIONS

1. Do you agree that *breadth* is the key to personal success abroad? Why or why not?
2. Are there any other traits, not mentioned above, that you think are important to success abroad? If so, what are they?
3. How would you rate yourself on the seven success traits mentioned above? Use the chart below.

	Excellent	Good	Fair	Poor
Hard like water	___	___	___	___
Resourceful independence through others	___	___	___	___
Curiosity	___	___	___	___
Positive regard for others	___	___	___	___
Emotional stability	___	___	___	___
Technical competence	___	___	___	___
Motivation	___	___	___	___

TEAM TASKS: PREPARING FOR THE INTERVIEWS

The final team task will involve interviewing for new job assignments overseas. Before the interviewing begins, the exact nature of the new overseas job assignments needs to be decided, e.g., a junior level marketing position in the U.S. Use the following form to help you clarify. Then teams will prepare for the interviews as directed below.

Job: Marketing/Finance/General Management/Operations/Other

Level: Senior / Mid-level / Junior

Company: (Specify) _____

Job Tasks: (Specify) _____

Country: U.S./Japan/France/Mexico/Saudi Arabia/Thailand/Other

Other Details: (Specify) _____

Form teams to prepare for the interviews. Each team will focus on one of the two tasks below.

1. Your team will interview several people and then choose the best person for the overseas job assignment. Your task now is to (1) establish your own criteria for the type of person you are looking for, (2) clarify interviewing roles and strategies that you will use, and (3) form a core set of questions that will help you in deciding whether and how well each person fits your criteria.
2. You will be interviewed, individually, for the overseas job assignment(s). Your task now is as a team to (1) discuss the main criteria that you think are important for the job(s) listed, (2) discuss effective strategies and tactics that interviewees can use to make good impressions with interviewers, (3) predict types of questions that the interviewers will ask and effective ways of answering those questions.

In addition to preparing for the interviews, it will be useful for one or two persons to observe, analyze, and later report on the general skills, strategies, questions, answers, etc. that are used in the interviews.

FINAL TEAM TASK: INTERVIEWS & ORAL REPORTS

1. Interview and be interviewed as the teacher instructs you. As you participate in this process, observe yourself and others.
2. For the interviewing teams, choose a representative to report (after the interviews) on your criteria, decisions and reasons for selecting the person you selected.
3. For those interviewed, be ready to report on your own strategies and observations during the interview process.

FINAL REPORT

Write a concise, yet thorough report on your decision (if you were an interviewer) or on your success or your observations (if you were an interviewee).

Segment 4

Walt Disney World Versus Universal Studios

from *Business World,* 8/5/90
Runtime: 6:22
Begin: 23:19

Previewing

KEY QUESTIONS

1. What do you look for when choosing where to go on vacation? What can vacation attraction companies do to encourage you to go to their attractions and not others?
2. How would you characterize the competition in your industry (or in an industry that you are interested in)?
3. What are the strengths, weaknesses, opportunities, and threats (S.W.O.T.) of one company in that industry?

DISCUSSION

1. What kind of activities and attractions do you prefer when you go on vacation? _____

   _____

2. What can companies which provide vacation activities and attractions do to encourage you to use their services rather than those of competitors?

   _____

   _____

PREDICTION

Based on the title of the segment, Walt Disney World Versus Universal Studios, and what you may already know about Walt Disney World and Universal Studio attractions, what information do you think will be included on the video?

1. _____

2. _____

3. _____

ESSENTIAL WORDS TO KNOW

The following words are used in the video. Read the sentences below. Then match the words to their meanings.

boom: In the 1970's, the oil industry experienced a *boom*, but that ended in the 1980's.

drought: We can survive a financial *drought* for about two years; after that, we may go bankrupt!

downturn: Higher travel prices could cause a *downturn* in the tourist industry, which has been very good until now.

gross (v): To be successful, a film has to *gross* over $50 million nowadays.

prompt (v): The high demand *prompted* the company to increase their production rate.

1. boom ___d___   a. financial decrease or reversal

2. drought ___e___   b. cause

3. downturn ___a___   c. bring in money (before expenses are paid)

4. gross ___c___   d. huge growth

5. prompt ___b___   e. long-lasting lack (of income or sales)

Global Viewing

TEAM QUESTIONING COMPETITION

23:19-
29:41

1. Form small teams to watch the video segment. Each team will develop five or more questions about the video that must be answered by a competing team. The questions should focus on the major details in the video and should be written down by the team's representative. These questions can focus on information in the video or that could be implied or applied from the video segment.

2. Read and listen to the first two minutes of the video. Generate the questions as a team. Do a quality control check on the team's questions to ensure that they make sense and can be understood by others.

3. Begin the competition. One person from each team asks one question of one person from another team. Any question that is correct and appropriate is worth one point. An answer that is correct and given within a specified time limit, e.g. 7 seconds, is worth two points for the answering team. A question that has already been asked and correctly answered receives no points; if the other team goes ahead and answers it, they receive two points. Bottom Line: Form solid questions on major details that the other team(s) are not likely to ask or to be able to answer.

QUESTIONS

1. _____
2. _____
3. _____
4. _____
5. _____
6. _____
7. _____
8. _____
9. _____
10. _____

Intensive Viewing

REVIEW & FILL IN THE BLANKS

24:05-
25:09

Return to the beginning of the video segment and review the first part of it, pausing several times to clarify points that are not generally understood. Then, beginning with Ken Prewitt's report (24:05-25:09), fill in the blanks below:

Tourists _go ape_ over new Universal Studios. That, at least, is what Universal officials in Orlando would like to be hearing this summer. In the city _best known_ for the Magic Kingdom, Disney rival Universal is betting $600 million that some of Disney's _magic_ will rub off.

The battle pits Disney with Walt Disney World, Epcot Center and its very successful Disney MGM Studio tour against Universal, just _12_ miles down the road – a battle of not only _substance_ but style.

While Disney has made its fortune selling _soft_ and cuddly, Universal is out to win, not by tender, but by _terror_.

Steve Lew: Nowhere else in the world except at Universal Studios in Florida can a visitor experience the three-dimensional, _interactive_, motion picture sensations that we offer. We put people in the _scene_, in the movie.

NOTETAKING

25:09-
29:41

Briefly look at the notetaking form below to prepare for your notetaking. Then view the rest of the video and take notes. When you finish, compare your notes with others to check your comprehension.

1. Universal's troubles: _mechanical breakdowns in its star attractions_
2. Universal's response to troubles: _rain checks_
3. Orlando's advantage over Hollywood: _Labor costs 1/3_
4. Universal's investment: _$600 million_
5. Universal's potential return on investment: _15-25% over 10 yrs._
6. Disney's movie division income: _$257 million_
7. Disney's theme parks' income: _$788 million_
8. Visitor days per year at Disney World: _33 million_
9. Visitor days per year at Sea World: _4 million_

10. Visitor days per year at Busch Gardens: _____ *3.5 mil*

11. Visitor days per year at Kennedy Space Center: _ *> 3 mil*

12. Universal's hope for visitor days per year: _____ *6 mil*

13. Visitors from foreign lands: _____ *25* %

14. Where most foreign visitors come from: ___ *Can. + Eur.*

15. Disney's strategy to boost income: *get vis. to stay longer*

16. Universal's strategies to boost market share: *3-D billboards on Rd to Dis. World, new kind of movie trailer (an ad placed before the movie).*

17. Anheuser-Busch' acquisition: _____ *Sea World*

18. Anheuser-Busch' marketing reputation: _ *Very aggressive*

19. Anheuser-Busch' specific marketing decision: *↑ advertising*

20. Potential losers in the marketing battle: _ *smaller attractions*

21. Lynn Hamilton-Foos' prediction of attendance drought: *3 yrs.*

Language Focus

MEANING FROM CONTEXT

Read the list of expressions below, and then watch the video again, listening for the expressions and how they are used by the speakers. After you hear the expression in context, try to write your own definition.

23:19-29:41

1. bet: _____ *gamble*

2. billboard: _____ *sign*

3. boost: _____ *increase*

4. dwarf (v): _____ *make something seem very small*

5. hit (n): _____ *success*

6. plagued by: _____ *troubled by*

7. rain check: _____ *promise something for a later date*

8. return on investment: _____ *profit*

Now fill in the missing words.

1. We ran out of the products on sale, so we gave our customers a _rain_ _check_ to buy the product next month at the sale price.
2. IBM's sales _dwarf_ those of its competitors.
3. If we risk investing in the stock market, we could get a higher _____ _return_ than if we put the money in a bank.
4. The company is trying to _boost_ sales by offering a discount for buying in volume.
5. That play was a _hit_ on Broadway; it sold more tickets than any other play last season.
6. In many large cities around the world, there are _billboards_ on the sides of buildings to advertise products.
7. By investing in real estate, they're _betting_ that the market will come back.
8. The U.S. auto industry has been _plagued_ rising labor costs and slow sales.

Postviewing

MAKING VISUAL AIDS

Using the information presented on the video, make two visual aids that attractively present the following information to a business audience:

1. One visual aid should present information on visitor days per year at each of the major attractions in central Florida.
2. The second visual aid should contrast the marketing tactics used by Disney, Universal, and Anheuser-Busch—as described on the video.

A READING ON MARKETING

Read the following excerpts from Philip Kotler's classic marketing text, *Marketing Management,* in preparation for the final team task.

External Environment Analysis (Opportunity and Threat Analysis)

The mission statement will help the business define its *environmental scanning* needs. The business manager now knows the parts of the environment to monitor and understand if the business is to achieve its objectives. In general, the company has to monitor key *macroenvironment forces* (demographic/economic, technological, political/legal, and social/cultural) that affect its business. And it must monitor significant *microenvironment actors* (customers, competitors, distribution channels, suppliers) that affect its ability to earn profits in this marketplace.

The business unit needs to categorize these environmental factors and set up a *marketing intelligence system* to track trends and important developments. Then, for each trend or development, the marketer should identify the obvious or not-so-obvious opportunities and threats.

Opportunities One of the major purposes of environmental scanning is to discern new opportunities. We define a company marketing opportunity as follows:

A company marketing opportunity is an attractive arena for company marketing action in which the company would enjoy a competitive advantage.

These opportunities should be classified according to their *attractiveness* and *success probability* that the company would have with each opportunity. The company's success probability with a particular opportunity depends on whether its *business strengths* (i.e., *distinctive competences*) not only match the *key success requirements* for operating in the target market but also exceed those of its competitors. The best-performing company will be the one that can generate the greatest customer value and sustain it over time. Having competence is not enough. The company must bring superior competence in order to attain a *sustainable competitive advantage.*

Threats Some of the developments in the external environment represent threats. We define an environmental threat as follows:

An environmental threat is a challenge posed by an unfavorable trend or development in the environment that would lead, in the absence of purposeful marketing action, to the erosion of the company's or industry's position.

The various identified threats should be classified according to their *seriousness* and *probability of occurrence.*

By assembling a picture of major threats and opportunities facing a specific business, it is possible to characterize its overall attractiveness. Four outcomes are possible. An *ideal business* is one that is high in opportunities and low or devoid of major threats. A *speculative business* is high in both major opportunities and threats. A *mature business* is low in major opportunities and threats. Finally, a *troubled business* is low in opportunities and high in threats.

Internal Environment Analysis (Strength and Weakness Analysis)

It is one thing to discern opportunities in the environment; it is another to have the necessary competencies to succeed in these opportunities. Each business needs to evaluate its strengths and weaknesses periodically. This can be done by using a form such as the one shown in Figure 2-12 [on page 45]. Each factor is rated as to whether is is a major strength, minor strength, neutral factor, minor weakness, or major weakness.

Of course, not all factors are equally important for succeeding in a business, or succeeding with a specific new marketing opportunity presented to this business. Therefore, it is also necessary to rate the importance of each factor—high, medium, or low—for the business as a whole or for a particular marketing opportunity.

This analysis tells us that even when a business has a major strength in a certain factor (i.e., a *distinctive competence*), that strength does not necessarily create a *competitive advantage*. First, it may not be a competence of any importance to the customers in that market. Second, even if it is, competitors may have the same strength level in that factor. What becomes important then, is for the business to have relatively greater strength in that factor than its competitors. Thus, two competitors may enjoy low manufacturing costs, but the one with the lower of the manufacturing costs has a competitive advantage.

Reprinted with Permission from Philip Kotler, *Marketing Management, Sixth Edition*, Prentice Hall, Chapter 2, pp. 50-54.

Fig. 2-12 Strengths and Weakness Analysis								
	Performance					Importance		
	Major	Minor	Neutral	Minor	Major	Hi	Med	Lo
Marketing Strength								
1. Company is well-known and highly regarded	___	___	___	___	___	__	__	__
2. Company has a strong relative market share	___	___	___	___	___	__	__	__
3. Good reputation for quality	___	___	___	___	___	__	__	__
4. Good reputation for service	___	___	___	___	___	__	__	__
5. Low manufacturing costs	___	___	___	___	___	__	__	__
6. Low distribution costs	___	___	___	___	___	__	__	__
7. Effective sales force	___	___	___	___	___	__	__	__
8. Effective R & D and innovation	___	___	___	___	___	__	__	__
9. Geographical advantage	___	___	___	___	___	__	__	__
10. Raw material advantage	___	___	___	___	___	__	__	__
Financial Strengths								
11. Low cost of capital	___	___	___	___	___	__	__	__
12. High availability	___	___	___	___	___	__	__	__
13. High profitability	___	___	___	___	___	__	__	__
14. Financial stability	___	___	___	___	___	__	__	__
Manufacturing Strengths								
15. New, well-equipped facilities	___	___	___	___	___	__	__	__
16. Strong economies of scale	___	___	___	___	___	__	__	__
17. Capacity to meet demand	___	___	___	___	___	__	__	__
18. Able and dedicated work force	___	___	___	___	___	__	__	__
19. Able to deliver on time	___	___	___	___	___	__	__	__
20. Technical and manufacturing skill	___	___	___	___	___	__	__	__
Organizational Strengths								
21. Enlightened, visionary leadership	___	___	___	___	___	__	__	__
22. Capable managers	___	___	___	___	___	__	__	__
23. Dedicated workforce	___	___	___	___	___	__	__	__
24. Entrepreneurial orientation	___	___	___	___	___	__	__	__
25. Flexible and adaptable	___	___	___	___	___	__	__	__
26. Speedy response to changing conditions	___	___	___	___	___	__	__	__

Reprinted with Permission from Philip Kotler, *Marketing Management, Sixth Edition*, Prentice Hall, Chapter 2, pp. 50-54.

MAKING MATRICES

In the original version of Kotler's text, three matrices are provided for the reader to describe the information given on page s 43 to 45. Using information from the text, reconstruct a matrix for each of the following: (1) opportunity, (2) threat, (3) performance-importance. Then think of a specific business situation and clearly and concisely explain what each cell in each matrix would mean to the business manager in that situation.

(1) Opportunity

(2) Threat

(3) Performance-Importance

FINAL TEAM TASK: S.W.O.T. ANALYSIS MEETING

Form two or more teams to work on this task. Each team will conduct a S.W.O.T. analysis on a different company's situation in the same industry, e.g., if one team worked on Disney, another would work on Universal, and perhaps another on Anheuser-Busch. Each member of each team should also evaluate the leadership and participants of the meeting as previously described in the instructions on pages 21 and 22 of Unit One, Segment 2 (after the class decides on the industry to focus on):

1. Select a team leader to run the meeting(s).
2. Select the company and gather as much information about that company as is feasible.
3. Conduct your S.W.O.T. (strength, weakness, opportunity, and threat) analysis of that company's situation. Be sure in your analysis to focus on a company's sustainable competitive advantage over its competitors. Use Figure 2-12 from Kotler's text when analyzing strengths, weaknesses, performance, and importance.
4. Design visual aids for your team to use in its presentation to the CEO (Chief Executive Officer). Make your visual aids as professional in appearance as possible.
5. Select two representatives to present your analysis.

S.W.O.T. ANALYSIS REPORT

Write a clear, concise report summarizing your S.W.O.T. analysis. Include some information in graphic form in your report.

Segment 5

Positioning Compaq in the PC Industry

from *Business World*, 5/6/90
Runtime: 4:14
Begin: 29:43

Previewing

KEY QUESTIONS

1. What are the key factors in buying and using a computer?
2. How does a small new company challenge the competition to ensure its own success?
3. What are the key factors for a company in positioning a product in the computer industry? In other specific industries?

DISCUSSION

1. What would the key factors be for you in buying and using a computer?

_____

_____

2. If you had the opportunity to start up a new personal computer company, how would you position your company and products, i.e., make them different from the competition so that consumers would buy your products?

_____

_____

_____

PREDICTION

Read the chart and the breif overview of Compaq Computer Corporation below. Then, combine your background knowledge, and the information learned from the segment title, the chart, and the overview, to predict the information you think will be included in the video segment.

The World's Largest Computer Companies (in terms of estimated information system sales—1989)	
IBM	$60,000,000,000+
Digital Equipment	$12,000,000,000+
NEC	$11,000,000,000+
Fujitsu	$11,000,000,000+
Unisys	$9,000,000,000+
Hitachi	$8,000,000,000+
Hewlett-Packard	$7,000,000,000+
Groupe Bull	$6,000,000,000+
Siemens	$6,000,000,000+
Olivetti	$5,000,000,000+
Apple	$5,000,000,000+
NCR	$5,000,000,000+
Toshiba	$4,000,000,000+
Canon	$3,000,000,000+
Matsushita	$3,000,000,000+
Compaq	$2,000,000,000+
AT&T / Philips / Nixdorf / Xerox-(each)	$2,000,000,000+

OVERVIEW OF COMPAQ COMPUTER CORP.

Houston's Compaq, the #1 maker of IBM-compatible computers, reached $1 billion in annual sales within 5 years, faster than any company in history. Unlike other IBM clone makers, ... Compaq conducts its own R&D and engineers many of its products instead of assembling other manufacturers' components. Compaq has a long list of innovations. It was first to develop a fully compatible IBM portable, first to successfully integrate a hard disk drive into a portable, and first with a monitor that displays both graphics and high-resolution text.

Compaq shipped its first computer in 1982... The company went public in 1983. ... Sales continued to skyrocket in the following years.... Compaq's success was due in part to its ability to hit the market with the right machine at the right time. In 1983 Compaq introduced a portable computer 18 months before IBM, and in 1986 it was first to market with a computer based on Intel's 386 chip.

Excerpted by permission from *Hoover's Handbook 1991: Profiles of Over 500 Major Corporation*, Copyright © 1990, The Reference Press, Inc., Austin, Texas. All rights reserved.

Now make predictions about what you think might be included in the video segment.

1. _____
2. _____
3. _____
4. _____
5. _____

Global Viewing

CONFIRMING YOUR PREDICTIONS

Watch the entire video segment. As you watch, put a check (✔) next to any of your predictions from the preview section that were mentioned.

29:43-
34:57

Prediction 1 _____

Prediction 2 _____

Prediction 3 _____

Prediction 4 _____

Prediction 5 _____

GETTING A FEEL FOR COMPAQ

Look at the checklist below and then watch the video. Focus on the items below. After viewing the video, check the appropriate responses. When you finish, compare your notes with others to check your comprehension.

29:43-
34:57

1. early 1990 earnings:	high	___	___	___	___	___	low
2. early 1990 growth:	high	___	___	___	___	___	low
3. corporate culture:	good	___	___	___	___	___	bad
4. company campus:	big	___	___	___	___	___	small
5. marketing skills:	good	___	___	___	___	___	bad
6. marketing philosophy:	better	___	___	___	___	___	cheaper
7. laptop market entry:	easy	___	___	___	___	___	difficult
8. late 1989 news:	good	___	___	___	___	___	bad
9. U.S. market growth:	fast	___	___	___	___	___	slow
10. Compaq's focus:	U.S.	___	___	___	___	___	global

Intensive Viewing

MINI-S.W.O.T. ANALYSIS

Perform a mini-S.W.O.T. analysis of Compaq from what you have learned from the video, filling in the grid below with the key information. Then use your general knowledge of the computer industry to add any other factors to the grid that could affect Compaq.

STRENGTHS	WEAKNESSES	OPPORTUNITIES	THREATS

LISTENING FOR DETAILS

29:43-
34:57

Listen again to the Compaq story for the following details:

1. First quarter earnings increase in 1990: _____ %

2. First quarter international increase in 1990: _____ %

3. The reason for growth, according to Mr. Vanocur: _____

_____

_____

4. Compaq's approach to decision-making: _____

5. Compaq's position on rewarding performance: _____

_____

6. Compaq's method of decision-making: _____

7. Name of Compaq's founder and leader in 1990: _____

8. Compaq's sales in its first operating year: _____

9. Compaq's sales six years later: _____

10. Number of workers at Compaq: _____

11. Action of the so-called Gang of Nine: _____

_____

12. Result of Gang of Nine's action: _____

13. 1989 mistakes: _____

_____

14. European location of Compaq factory: _____

15. Compaq's place in European PC sales: _____

16. Mr. Canion's view of Compaq going into the next year: _____

_____

Language Focus

IN YOUR OWN WORDS

Read the following sentences from the video segment and then write short definitions or explanations of the italicized words.

1. At a time when other computer makers are *being squeezed*, why is Compaq still growing?

   being squeezed = _____

2. The answer may lie beyond technology and marketing, in a *corporate culture* that gives employees free Cokes and puts trees in the plants.

   corporate culture = _____

3. It's building team spirit and then really *cultivating* it, really rewarding team work as opposed to rewarding individual *performance*.

   cultivating = _____

   performance = _____

4. Compaq is a technology *powerhouse*, and a very *savvy* marketing organization. They have been able to position themselves out of the center of the PC business.

   powerhouse = _____

   savvy = _____

5. Our strategy has always been to offer the *enhanced functionality*, enhanced performance, either at the same price, or in many cases—in many respects, at a higher price than the competition.

   enhanced functionality = _____

53

6. Compaq (led) computer makers who successfully challenged IBM's decision ...Compaq also *went after* IBM in corporate sales, *making* sufficient *inroads* with its desktop machines in the mid-80's, so that it found easy *entry* for its laptops when it went after that market a few years later.

went after = _____

making inroads = _____

entry = _____

7. They introduced all these new products, but they didn't deliver them as quickly as they had expected or in as high a volume as they had expected, so that created a *glitch* in their earnings.

glitch = _____

8. Compaq is also under pressure from its dealers, whose *margins* have been squeezed, potentially a serious problem since Compaq relies *solely* on its dealer network for sales, a *concept* it pioneered.

margins = _____

solely = _____

concept = _____

Postviewing

TRACKING COMPAQ

Late 1991 Update: Much has changed at Compaq since this news report was broadcast. In1990, Compaq continued to increase both revenues and profits substantially. However, in 1991, with a recession in the U.S., revenues and profits dropped sharply. The company laid off over 1400 employees and reported its first loss ever, $70 million for the third quarter. Compaq's co-founder and leader, Rod Canion, was fired in October, 1991.

Your assignment: Search the periodicals, i.e., newspapers and business magazines for more recent news about Compaq. Then write an executive summary (one page or less) updating us on Compaq's position as in the example below.

IMPROVING BUSINESS LISTENING

Listening in business is an active process and a critical skill. Check the spaces below that best describe you, in general (G) and in meetings (M), and then discuss ways in which you could improve your business listening skills.

	GOOD G / M	FAIR G / M	WEAK G / M
1. I am generally patient when listening to someone. I do not interrupt frequently.			
2. I make the speaker feel comfortable. I show interest in what the speaker says.			
3. I ask questions to clarify and summarize, not to criticize or be judgmental.			
4. I concentrate on the important ideas. I do not get easily distracted.			
5. I generally understand the main ideas. I do not misinterpret what the speaker says.			
6. I maintain eye contact and avoid distracting body movement and gestures.			
7. I keep my emotions balanced. I do not get too emotional or emotionless in listening.			
8. I listen for feelings as well as facts. I am sensitive to things the speaker does not say, but may express through body language or tone or voice.			

9. Other tendencies I have in listening: _____

_____

_____

Ways I could improve my listening skills: _____

_____

_____

_____

_____

Read the following excerpts from Philip Kotler's classic marketing text, *Marketing Management*, and then fill in the outline following the excerpts.

Sellers can take three approaches to a market. Mass marketing is the decision to mass-produce and mass-distribute one product and attempt to attract all kinds of buyers. Product-variety marketing is the decision to produce two or more market offers differentiated in style, features, quality, sizes, and so on, and designed to offer variety to the market and distinguish the seller's products from competitors' products. Target marketing is the decision to distinguish the different groups that make up a market and to develop corresponding products and marketing mixes for each target market. Sellers today are moving away from mass marketing and product differentiation toward target marketing because the latter is more helpful in spotting market opportunities and developing effective products and marketing mixes.

The key steps in target marketing are market segmentation, market targeting, and product positioning. Market segmentation is the act of dividing a market into distinct groups of buyers who might merit separate products and/or marketing mixes. The marketer tries different variables to see which reveal the best segmentation opportunities. For consumer marketing, the major segmentation variables are geographic, demographic (age and lifestyle stage, sex, income), psychographic (social class, lifestyle, personality), and behavioral (occasions, benefits, user status, usage rate, loyalty status, buyer readiness stage, attitude). Industrial markets can be segmented by demographic variables, operating variables, purchasing approaches, situational factors, and personal characteristics. For each potential segment, a customer segment profile is developed. The effectiveness of the segmentation analysis depends on arriving at segments that are measurable, substantial, accessible, and actionable.

Next, the seller has to target the best market segment(s). To do this, the seller must first evaluate the profit potential of each segment. This is a function of segment size and growth, segment structural attractiveness..., and company objectives and resources.

This market targeting determines the company's competitors. The company must research the competitors' positions and decide on its best positioning. Positioning is the act of designing the company's image and value offer so that the segment's customers understand and appreciate what the company stands for in relation to its competitors. The positioning task consists of three steps: identifying possible competitive advantages to exploit, selecting the right ones, and effectively signaling to the market the firm's chosen position. The company's product-positioning strategy will then enable it to take the next step, namely, plan its competitive marketing strategies.

Many positions are available to a firm. It might go after the "low-price position," "high-quality position," "high-service position," "advanced-technology position" and so on. Essentially the firm is trying to establish a competitive advantage that it hopes will appeal to a substantial number of the segment's customers. Some firms will find it easy to choose their positioning strategy. Thus a firm that is well known for quality in other segments will go for this position in a new segment as long as there is a sufficient number of quality-oriented buyers. But in many cases, two or more firms will go after the same positioning. Then each will have to seek further differentiation, such as "high quality for a lower cost," or "high quality with more technical service." Another way of saying this is that each firm must build a unique bundle of competitive advantages that appeal to a substantial group within the segment. (p.308)

Reprinted with permission from Philip Kotler, *Marketing Management, Sixth Edition*, Prentice Hall, Chapter 10, p. 308 and 315-316

I. Three Approaches to Market:

    A. _____

    B. _____

    C. _____

II. Key Steps in Target Marketing:

    A. _____

    1. Consumer market variables:

        a. g _____

        b. d _____

        c. p _____

        d. b _____

    B. _____

    C. _____

    a. First step: _____

    b. Second step: _____

    c. Third step: _____

III. Examples of Product Positions:

    A. _____

    B. _____

    C. _____

    D. _____

    E. _____

    F. _____

FINAL TEAM TASK: MARKET SEGMENTATION & PRODUCT POSITIONING MEETING

Form two or more teams to work on this task. Each team will work on a different consumer product, e.g., personal computer, automobile, toothpaste, stereo equipment, hotel service, etc. Each member of each team should remain aware of the listening skills of all meeting participants and then evaluate those skills after the meeting.

Instructions:

1. Decide on your product or product category.
2. Decide on what company you represent.
3. Segment the market for your product, using whichever variables (geographic, demographic, psychographic, and/or behavioral) seem to fit best. Identify from three to nine different market segments. [For example, one could use two factors, e.g., age (teenagers, young adults, mature adults) and income (low, medium, high) and form a 9-cell matrix. That might not be the best way to segment your particular market. You need to study the market carefully.]
4. Discuss and decide on which segment(s) your team should target.
5. Discuss and decide on which competitive advantages your product has. Then select those advantages that give your product its best possible positioning.
6. Design a matrix or other type of exhibit which clearly indicates your product's position in relation to its competitors. That is, design a matrix based on main positioning strategies, and then place your product in it along with your competitors.
7. Give a formal presentation, with visual aids, on your team's work. The presentation should show the what and whys of your market segmentation, targeting, and positioning.

EXECUTIVE SUMMARY

Write a clear and concise report on your product's market segmentation, targeting, and positioning.

Segment 6

Sneaker Wars: Nike vs. Reebok

from *20/20*, 8/19/88
Runtime: 15:21
Begin: 35:02

Previewing

KEY QUESTIONS

1. What factors are most important to you when you buy relatively inexpensive consumer products?
2. How is marketing like warfare? Is warfare a good analogy for marketing? Why or why not?
3. How can you analyze the market and competitive environment to help you achieve greater marketing success?

DISCUSSION

1 How many pairs of sneakers (and sports shoes) do you own? _____

2. Why did you buy one brand over another brand, i.e., what factors were most important to you, e.g., advertisements, image, friends' advice, etc. _____
_____

3. In making decisions about much more expensive purchases, such as a computer, a car, or an overseas vacation package, what factors are the most important for you:

FACTOR	COMPUTER	CAR	VACATION
Price	_____	_____	_____
Friends' advice	_____	_____	_____
Advertisements	_____	_____	_____
Company's image	_____	_____	_____
Product features	_____	_____	_____

Other factors specific to each purchase:

_____	_____	_____	_____
_____	_____	_____	_____

PREDICTION

1. In the video, Nike's advertising slogan is "Just do it" while Reebok's is "U.B.U." (You be you). What differences, if any, in company marketing strategies do these slogans suggest? _____

    _____

2. Based on the title, *"Sneaker Wars: Nike vs. Reebok,"* and what you already know about the companies and the industry, what information do you think will be included in the video segment?

    a. _____

    b. _____

    c. _____

    d. _____

    e. _____

Global Viewing

CONFIRMING YOUR PREDICTION

35:02-
50:23

Watch the entire video segment. As you watch, put a check (✔) next to any of your predictions from the Preview section that were mentioned.

Prediction 1 _____

Prediction 2 _____

Prediction 3 _____

Prediction 4 _____

Prediction 5 _____

THE PHENOMENON

35:02-
38:02

Watch the first part of the video and fill in the grid below:

SNEAKER USERS	REASONS FOR USING SNEAKERS
_____	_____
_____	_____
_____	_____

Intensive Viewing

THE INDUSTRY AND THE COMPETITORS

Look over the grid below. Then watch the next part of the video and fill in the grid with the appropriate information. Compare your notes with others to check your comprehension when you finish.

38:02-
39:49

I. INDUSTRY

   A. Recent growth pattern: _____skyrocketing_____

   B. Annual sales at retail level: _____$6 billion_____

   C. Number of branded companies: _____20-25_____

   D. Number of companies with $50,000,000 annual sales: _10-12_

   E. Combined market share of Nike & Reebok: _over 50%_

II. COMPETITORS: <u>NIKE</u>   <u>REEBOK</u>

   A. Success based on

      1. shoe type   _performance_   _recreational_

      2. activity/lifestyle: _jogging/fitness_ _leisure_

   B. Decade of initial success: _70's_   _80's_

   C. Market share fight is over: _substance_ vs. _style_

THE NEW IDEA AND THE MISTAKE

Watch the next two minutes of the video and fill in the grid below:

39:49-
42:06

1. The new idea: _____aerobics shoes_____

2. The boss' first reaction: _____negative_____

3. The idea's effect on the industry: _changed it dramatically_

4. The mistake: _shoe w/ wrinkled toes_

5. The impact of the mistake: _Reebok + consumers loved it_

SUMMARIZING & COMMENTING

In either written or spoken form, briefly summarize the information given about the new idea and the manufacturing mistake. Then comment on both. Are they typical situations in business? What, if anything, can others learn from Reebok's experiences here?

THE LEADERS

Watch the next part of the video and compare and contrast the two leaders, Paul Fireman of Reebok and Philip Knight of Nike:

42:06-44:28

CHARACTERISTIC	PAUL FIREMAN *Reebok*	PHILIP KNIGHT *Nike*
1. What he did before founding the company:	salesman / mgr sporting goods	middle dist. runner
2. Preferred sport now:	golf	tennis
3. Last year's income:	15,500,000	↑
4. Descriptive adjectives: (in your own words)	calm relaxed smooth	intense (not given) competitive serious

SEQUENCING THE EVENTS

44:28-50:23

Watch the rest of the video. Then put the events below into the correct chronological order, that is, mark #1 for the event that happened first, #2 for the event that followed, and so on.

_3_ Reebok's first big success.

_2_ Mistake in Reebok's Korean factory.

_5_ Michael Jordan's $19,000,000 endorsement contract.

_1_ Keds and Converse—the big names in the sneaker industry.

_6_ L.A. Gear's big push in the competitive arena.

_X_ L.A. Gear decides to rely on massive research and development.

_4_ The Air Revolution visible airbag shoe by Nike comes out.

Language Focus

WORD CHECK

Match the words from the video with the words/phrases that follow:

1. get underway _c_
2. counter (v) _f_
3. soft sell _a_
4. mystique _b_
5. obsession _e_
6. fashion statement _d_

a. persuade in a gentle manner
b. unusual and positive image
c. begin
d. status symbol
e. something people are crazy about
f. fight back

IMPORTANT SALES AND MARKETING TERMS

The following words are important terms used in sales and marketing. Read each word and its brief definition. Then write your own sentence for each of the *italicized* words.

1. *consumer* = a person who buys or uses a product

_____

_____

2. *demographics* = information about a market

_____

_____

3. *driving force* = a leader or person who is behind something, trying to make it successful

_____

_____

4. *emerge* = come out

_____

_____

5. *gimmick* = a strategy or scheme to promote a product

_____

_____

6. *hit the jackpot* = be very successful; make a lot of money

_____

_____

7. *momentum* = a steadily rising increase in something (i.e., sales, profits)

_____

_____

8. *skyrocket* (v) = soar; increase very quickly

_____

_____

Postviewing

MINI-S.W.O.T. ANALYSIS

Perform a mini-S.W.O.T. analysis on both Nike and Reebok, based on what you've learned from the video, filling in the grid below with the key information. Then use your general knowledge of the sneaker industry to add any other factors to the grid that could affect the companies.

	STRENGTHS	WEAKNESSES	OPPORTUNITIES	THREATS
Nike:				
Reebok:				

PRODUCT POSITIONING MATRIX

Put the names of Nike, Reebok, L.A. Gear, and other sneaker companies you know of in the appropriate places in the matrix below.

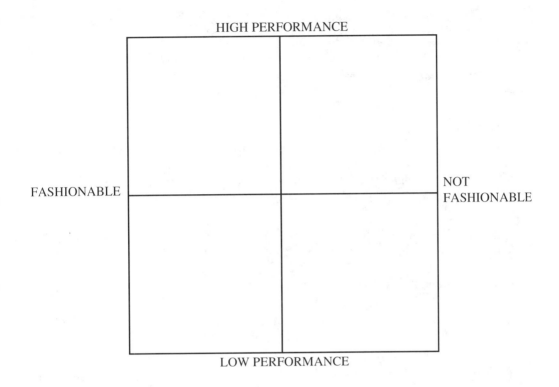

TRACKING THE COMPANIES

Search the business periodicals and reference materials for more recent developments about Nike & Reebok. If you have time, also check news about what happened to L.A. Gear. Then write an executive summary (one page or less) updating us on and comparing the companies' positions in the market, sales records, new products, new marketing efforts, and so on.

READING ON MARKETING WARFARE

Read the following excerpts from *Marketing Warfare* by Ries and Trout, and then answer the questions below it.

Introduction: Marketing is War

Being customer-oriented

Marketing people traditionally have been customer-oriented. Over and over again they have warned management to be customer-oriented rather than production-oriented.

Ever since World War II, King Customer has reigned supreme in the world of marketing.

But it's beginning to look like King Customer is dead. And like marketing people have been selling a corpse to top management.

Companies who have dutifully followed the directions of their marketing experts have seen millions of dollars disappear in valiant but disastrous customer-oriented efforts.

To see how we got into this predicament, you have to go back to the twenties when business was production-oriented. This was the heyday of Henry "You Can Have Any Color You Want As Long As It's Black" Ford.

In the production era, business discovered advertising. "Mass advertising creates mass demand which makes mass production possible," said the advertising experts.

In the aftermath of World War II, the leading companies became customer-oriented. The marketing expert was in charge and the prime minister was marketing research.

But today every company is customer-oriented. Knowing what a customer wants isn't too helpful if a dozen other companies are already serving the same customer's wants....

Becoming competitor-oriented

To be successful today, a company must become competitor-oriented. It must look for weak points in the positions of its competitors and then launch marketing attacks against those weak points. Many recent marketing success stories illustrate this.

For example, while others were losing millions in the computer business, Digital Equipment Corporation was making millions by exploiting IBM's weakness in small computers.

Similarly, Savin established a successful beachhead in small, inexpensive copiers, a weak point in the Xerox lineup.

And Pepsi took advantage of its sweeter taste to challenge Coke in the hotly contested cola market. At the same time, Burger King was making progress against McDonald's with its "broiling, not frying" attack.

There are those who would say that a well-thought-out marketing plan always includes a section on the competition. Indeed it does. Usually at the back of the plan in a section entitled "Competitive Evaluation." The major part of the plan usually spells out the marketplace, its various segments, and a myriad of customer research statistics carefully gleaned from endless focus groups, test panels and concept and market tests.

The marketing plan of the future

In the marketing plan of the future, many more pages will be dedicated to the competition. This plan will carefully dissect each participant in the marketplace. It will develop a list of competitive weaknesses and strengths as well as a plan of action to either exploit or defend against them.

There might even come a day when this plan will contain a dossier on each of the competitor's key marketing people which will include their favorite tactics and style of operation (not unlike the documents the Germans kept on Allied commanders in World War II).

What does this portend for marketing people of the future?

It means they have to be prepared to wage marketing warfare.

More and more, successful marketing campaigns will have to be planned like military campaigns.

Strategic planning will become more and more important. Companies will have to learn how to attack and to flank their competition, how to defend their positions, and how and when to wage guerrilla warfare. They will need better intelligence on how to anticipate competitive moves.

On the personal level, successful marketing people will have to exhibit many of the same virtues that make a great military general— courage, loyalty, and perserverence.

Maybe Clausewitz is right

Maybe marketing is war, where the competition is the enemy and the objective is to win the battle.

Principles of defensive marketing warfare.
1. Only the market leader should consider playing defense.
2. The best defensive strategy is the courage to attack yourself.
3. Strong competitive moves should always be blocked.

Principles of offensive marketing warfare.
1. The main consideration is the strength of the leader's position.
2. Find a weakness in the leader's strength and attack at that point.
3. Launch an attack on as narrow a front as possible.

Principles of flanking marketing warfare.
1. A good flanking move must be made into an uncontested area.
2. Tactical surprise ought to be an important element in the plan.
3. The pursuit is as critical as the attack itself.

Principles of guerrilla marketing warfare.
1. Find a segment of the market small enough to defend.
2. No matter how successful you become, never act like the leader.
3. Be prepared to bugout at a moment's notice.

1. What is the main idea of the passage? _____

   _____

2. What is the problem with being customer-oriented in today's
   marketplace, according to the authors? _____

   _____

3. What do the authors recommend as the key idea in successful marketing
   in the future? _____

   _____

4. Why do the authors use the military analogy in their book on
   business marketing? _____

   _____

5. What companies mentioned in the passage are market leaders
   (in other words, which companies are others trying to attack)?

   _____, _____, _____, _____

6. What companies mentioned in the passage are market challengers?

   _____, _____, _____, _____

7. How would you describe Nike and Reebok in these terms?
   Nike is _____/Reebok is _____

8. What words in the passage associated with warfare are used to describe
   marketing actions? (Hint: There are more than 10 such words)

   _____

   _____

   _____

9. Now use five words from the above list to describe a marketing action.
   Use one word per sentence.

   a. _____

   b. _____

   c. _____

   d. _____

   e. _____

10. Do you agree with the ideas presented in the passage? Why or why not?

    _____

    _____

COMPARING PRODUCTS

List the major competitors in one or more consumer product industries. Examples of products you could discuss include TVs, VCRs, watches, cameras, sports equipment, stereo equipment, soap, cold relief medicine, etc. Then discuss how they compete with each other in terms of product differences, market segments, & product positioning.

INDUSTRY	1	2	3	4
(Type of products) _____	_____	_____	_____	
COMPANIES: _____	_____	_____	_____	
_____	_____	_____	_____	
_____	_____	_____	_____	
_____	_____	_____	_____	
_____	_____	_____	_____	
_____	_____	_____	_____	
_____	_____	_____	_____	

FINAL TEAM TASK: PRODUCT, CONSUMER, & COMPETITOR RESEARCH

Your team will act as consultants for one consumer products company. You will do research outside the class and then work together to give a sophisticated presentation about your project. Included in your work will be information gathering and analysis of market segmentation, product benefits according to consumer preferences, and competitor strengths and weaknesses. You will need to do the following:

1. Decide which consumer product you will research. Decide which company is your client for this project.
2. Gather as much information about the various companies that produce the product as you can. Useful information includes company size compared to its competitors, market share, growth rate, profitability, etc. You can get this from annual reports, library reference materials, business magazine articles, and so on.
3. Also gather as much information about the various brands of the product that the company produces. You can get this from magazine ads, consumer magazines, brochures, retail store clerks, and so on.
4. Develop a form which you can use to compare the information you have and to gather more information. For example, if you wanted to look at basketball shoes, you might develop a form like this:

	Brand 1	Brand 2	Brand 3	Brand 4
Price	_____	_____	_____	_____
Features	_____	_____	_____	_____
Colors	_____	_____	_____	_____
Technology	_____	_____	_____	_____
Performance	_____	_____	_____	_____
Other	_____	_____	_____	_____

5. Do your product research by going to a store in your area.
6. Develop a concise questionnaire about your consumer product. Include questions about what brands people buy, why they buy those particular brands, how much they buy, how often, where, when, etc. You may want to get basic information on each respondent, such as age, sex, occupation, other characteristics. You can do part of this by observing the people and the rest by asking questions. Be careful to form questions that are polite, yet yield the information you want.
7. Interview as many people as you can.
8. Analyze your product, consumer, and competitor data and come up with the following types of charts to use in your presentation to the Chief Executive Officer (CEO):

BENEFIT ANALYSIS: Rank order each benefit as it is desired by each segment, e.g., for sneakers, athletes might rank performance #1 while middle-age wearers might rank comfort #1.

Top Benefits Desired by Consumers	Segment A	Segment B	Segment C
1. _____	_____	_____	_____
2. _____	_____	_____	_____
3. _____	_____	_____	_____
4. _____	_____	_____	_____
5. _____	_____	_____	_____

COMPETITIVE ANALYSIS: Rank each competitor on each of the top benefits (from the chart on page 70).For example, for sneakers, Nike might rank #1 in performance while Reebok might rank #1 in style. Use the benefits you came up with in your benefit analysis.

Main Competitors:	Benefits:	1	2	3	4	5
Your client		___	___	___	___	___
_____		___	___	___	___	___
_____		___	___	___	___	___
_____		___	___	___	___	___
_____		___	___	___	___	___

COMPETITOR STRENGTHS/WEAKNESSES BY SEGMENT
This chart basically combines the previous two by looking at consumer preferences and competitor strengths in each segment. Once this information is obtained, your team should have a fairly clear idea of how your client can best position its products in each segment.

9. Design several product positioning matrices that illustrate the key features of the competition at the present time.
10. Decide on a simple marketing action plan with your recommendations for your client. Your action plan should contain the following parts:
    a. Objectives
    b. Strategy and tactics (relate your recommendations to the principles of marketing warfare described earlier). Here you should include key market segments to target, your priorities, and changes in product positioning.
11. Prepare a sophisticated presentation summarizing your team's effort. Prepare visual aids that effectively illustrate your main findings.
12. Practice your presentation. Time your practice sessions and trim your presentation to fit the requirements of your learning situation. Also use this time to focus on your team's ability to communicate clearly, concisely, informatively, and persuasively.
13. Present your oral report to the CEO.

FINAL REPORT

Write a clear, concise informative, and persuasive report that summarizes your team's conclusions. Include exhibits that clearly and attractively illustrate your main findings.

Segment 7

High Tech into the 90s

from *Business World,* 12/31/89
Runtime: 11:12
Begin: 50:28

Previewing

KEY QUESTIONS

1. What new products have been developed in the last 30 years?
2. What are the new trends that will affect business and people's lives in the next decade and beyond?
3. What types of innovations might come about in the next 10 years? 30 years?
4. What changes will occur in people's lives and in the business world if these innovations do occur?

NEW PRODUCTS FROM MORE THAN 30 YEARS AGO

Special Research Assignment: Find out when each of the following products first came to market in the world. If possible, also find out when each was first conceived and figure out how many years it took from conception to realization. Then write a clear and concise executive summary on your findings.

PRODUCT	FIRST YEAR ON MARKET	YEAR CONCEIVED	TOTAL TIME TO MARKET
antibiotics	_____	_____	_____
automobile	_____	_____	_____
ball point pen	_____	_____	_____
cellophane	_____	_____	_____
pacemaker	_____	_____	_____
instant coffee	_____	_____	_____

PRODUCT	FIRST YEAR ON MARKET	YEAR CONCEIVED	TOTAL TIME TO MARKET
liquid shampoo	_____	_____	_____
mainframe computers	_____	_____	_____
motion pictures	_____	_____	_____
nylon	_____	_____	_____
radar	_____	_____	_____
television	_____	_____	_____
Xerox copiers	_____	_____	_____

DISCUSSION

1. Form a team and then list as many *specific* product or service innovations, that is, brand new products, as you can that have come to market in the last 30 years. The personal computer is one such example. Some areas where innovations have occurred include airlines, banking, clothing and footwear, communications, container technology, energy, entertainment and image technology, food products and processes, information technology, medicine, office products, personal care products, production technology, shelter, and transportation.

_____ _____ _____

_____ _____ _____

_____ _____ _____

_____ _____ _____

_____ _____ _____

2. a. Look at each innovation individually and then decide how it changed the business and/or personal lives of the people it affected, e.g., convenience, quality, speed, safety, lifestyle, etc. If you run out of space on this page, use another piece of paper.

NEW PRODUCT HOW IT CHANGED THINGS

_____ _____

_____ _____

_____ _____

_____ _____

_____ _____

b. In what ways do these products most commonly change business or people's lives? _____

_____

_____

3. Have one or two representatives from your team present your ideas to the larger class. Use visual aids if possible.

PREDICTION

Based on the title of the segment, *High Tech into the 90's*, what information do you think will be included in the video segment?

1. _____

2. _____

3. _____

4. _____

Global Viewing

WHAT WAS & WHAT'S NEXT?

Read the chart below. As you view the video segment, focus only on what is said about computers in the 80's and computers in the 90's to fill in the missing information.

50:28-
1:01:40

POINT RAISED	IN THE 80'S	IN THE 90's	
1. Computer location:	stationary	anywhere	
2. Emphasis in office:	collecting data	managing data	integrating info.
3. Software shift:	personal productivity	networking +connectivity	+data access
4. Focus:	data	images	
5. Desktop change:	business tool	info. assistant	
6. Work location:	office	home	
7. Decade of the:	employer	employee	
8. Home computer in:	den	kitchen	

75

COMPARING NOTES & DECADES

Compare your notes with others to check your comprehension. Then discuss whether each of the changes noted above is happening (or will happen) as the computer experts have predicted. If you have no ideas about a particular issue, move on to the next one.

IS IT CHANGING?/WILL IT?   EVIDENCE

1. Computer location: _____

2. Emphasis in office: _____

3. Software shift: _____

4. Focus: _____

5. Desktop change: _____

6. Work location: _____

7. Decade of the: _____

8. Home location: _____

Intensive Viewing

LISTENING FOR DETAILS

50:28-
1:01:40

Look at the questions below and then watch the video segment again, answering the questions as you listen.

1. What is the enabling technology for the massive changes predicted?
   a micro processor chip

2. What is noted to be the most fundamental change and revolution that will happen in the 90's? _Group ware_

3. What will it allow people to do? _Work on same project 7 diff. computers_

4. Who will benefit the most from video-conferencing and computer conferencing? _Middle-level engineers_

5. Why? _Can save travel-time on projects_

6. What can the Idea Fisher program let you do? _Brainstorm_

7. What can the Grid Tablet do? _Recognize handwriting_

8. What is the #1 reason given for the decade of the employee?
   Demographics — intense labor shortages, aided by technology

9. What obstacle is noted that might delay one of the changes noted in the video? _Phone system — not enough fiber optic cables_

EXECUTIVE SUMMARY

Write a clear and concise summary (equal in length to one typed page) of the video segment. Be sure to include a comparison of the 80's and 90's and your comments on the accuracy of the video report and on the consequences for your business or work life if it is correct.

Language Focus

VOCABULARY CHECK

Read the short passages below. Watch the video again, listening for the sentence below. After each sentence write your own definition for the *italicized* word.

50:28-
1:01:40

1. Few of us could have predicted 10 years ago the *incredible* impact that changes in technology have had on the way we live and the way we work

   incredible: *unbelievable or massive*

2. What's next? ...I see the *emerging* of satellite communication, satellite telephone capabilities, paging systems, and computing.

   emerging: *Coming or developing*

3. Basically what's happening in the micro processor side of the business is that we are going to be able to have a Cray on your lap. So a lap Cray will be *feasible* as we approach the end of the decade.

   feasible: *practical*

4. I think in the 1990's the focus will be on *integrating* this information so we don't provide lots of separate information.

   integrating: _____

5. In the 90's the *emphasis* will be on not only accessing information but also accessing the information sources.

   emphasis: _____

6. One way to expand *networking* will be with group-ware, like the Lotus product Notes, which will allow people working on different computers to work on a project *simultaneously*.

   networking: _____

   simultaneously: _____

7. The *well-publicized* Next Computer from Steve Jobs features both multiple video windows and digital sound.

well-publicized: _____

8. By and large, the 90's, primarily because of the *demographics*, but also aided by the technology, is going to be the decade of the employee....
A very *dramatic* shift is occurring, propelled by the demographics, the very *intense* shortages, but aided by the fact that technology allows more *options*.

demographics: _____

dramatic: _____

intense: _____

options: _____

9. One of the biggest *obstacles* to getting the new technologies is the phone system, which might not have the fiber optics cables needed to transmit pictures into homes and offices until the 21st Century.

obstacles: _____

PREPARATION FOR THE MEETING: WAYS OF DISCUSSING THE FUTURE

This segment focuses on predicting what will happen in the future. To prepare for the final team task, look over each way of discussing the future, italicized below, that was mentioned in the video. Then use the word(s) in a new sentence that discusses the future. Try to use the same basic sentence structure as the examples provided below.

1　The new technologies *promise* to let you work smarter and friendlier and do it all from home. _____

_____

2. We *predict* that changes in technology *will* have an incredible impact on the way we live and the way we work. _____

_____

3. You will *expect* in the 90's *that* wherever you are, in an automobile, in an airplane, at home, at the office, that you are going to be part of the information system. _____

_____

4. I *see* the emerging of satellite communication, satellite telephone capabilities... _____

_____

5. Basically *what's happening* in the micro processor side of the business is that we *are going to* be able to have a Cray literally on top of your lap.

_____

_____

6. I *think* in the 1990s *the focus will be on* integrating this information so we don't provide lots of information that we don't need.

_____

_____

7. In the 90s, the *emphasis* will be on not only accessing information but also accessing the information sources. _____

_____

8. I *think* group-ware *is probably the most fundamental change* and revolution *that will happen* in the 90s. _____

_____

9. *If you want to* exchange documents or even video, *you'll be able to do so* with the new software. _____

_____

10. For business, *the new* technologies *mean you won't have to* be there to work there. _____

_____

11. *I'm going to expect to* talk to my computer, I'm going to expect that it's going to talk to me.... _____

_____

12. *The whole idea* of business at home and doing significantly more work at home *will finally come into play*. _____

_____

Postviewing

Read the following excerpts from an article by Barbara Jorgensen about one example of high tech into the 90's and then fill in the grid below it.

Home automation finally arrives

After a long string of costly, time-consuming false starts, home automation [HA] is here. The vision, according to HA developers, goes something like this:

The harried homeowner rushes off to work, leaving the coffee maker on, the VCR unprogrammed for that daytime show, and the security system deactivated. But once at work, she can use a touch-tone phone to turn off the coffee maker—(if it's not already programmed to do so), activate the VCR and security system, and even program the air conditioner to have the house at a pleasant 72 degrees by 6 P.M. The "smart house" might also turn off the lawn sprinkler in the event of rain and run the dishwasher once the laundry is finished.

Prototypes of such homes, backed by several partnerships and organizations, already exist. But by the end of this year—for the first time since the smart house was envisioned a decade ago—several new protocols (or technological systems) will bring an unprecedented level of automation to existing and future homes, apartments, and industrial buildings....

Reaping many of the rewards of the smart house will be semiconductor makers such as Texas Instruments, Motorola, and Toshiba. But payoffs also will flow to manufacturers of electrical and electronic components, control devices, security systems, computer hardware and software, communications equipment, and appliances.

The result: a $5.6 billion market for HA-compatible equipment by the year 2000, predicts Rose Associates, a Los Altos, Calif.-based market research firm. That figure includes hardware and software products for multifunction control systems, user interfaces such as phones and TVs, and communication networks, as well as subsystem markets for security and environmental-control products and services. Researchers at New York-based Frost and Sullivan Inc. predict that annual growth rates will rise from 1.2% last year to 35.4% by 2000.

...Regardless of how simple or sophisticated they happen to be, HA systems will depend heavily on semiconductors. Rose Associates predicts that the market for those chips...will grow from $163 million in 1990 to $328 by 1995 and then nearly double again to $628 million by 2000.

1. Innovation: Home automation
2. What it can do: _____
                      _____
                      _____
                      _____
                      _____
                      _____

3. Why the industry may grow: _____
4. The key industry in its future: _____
5. Your thoughts: Is this prediction realistic or too optimistic? Why?

   _____

   _____

RELATED READING 2

Read the following article and fill in the missing information in the
notetaking outline which follows.

Trends in the U.S. in the 90's and Beyond

As we go through the 90's, the changes that are occurring in many life situations
and lifestyles in the United States are quite dramatic. The changes are resulting not
only from simple demographic trends, e.g., the fact that the large Baby Boom
generation has now become a Graying Boom, but also from changes in technology,
economic conditions, and from the consequences of work and lifestyle changes in
the previous decades.

One demographic trend that has been going on for some time now is the low
birthrate in the country. The result of having fewer babies around has become a
threat to the business of some baby product manufacturers. They have had to come
up with new strategies to use and new markets to enter to keep their firms healthy.

A trend related both to the low birthrate and longer lifespans is the aging of
America, with increases in the numbers of advancing middle-age (40's and early
50's) and retirement age (over 65), with decreases in the numbers of certain other
age groups, e.g., late teens and early 20's. This points to new opportunities for some
types of products, declines for others, and changes in product packaging to cater to
the needs of the larger markets. An example of one change is the increased use of
large type on packages designed to appeal to more mature buyers.

Family-related trends in the last 10-20 years, such as large increases in two-
income families, where the wives work outside the home, and increased divorce
rates, with the resulting single-parent homes, have also had a big impact on the
demand for certain types of products. One example has been the explosion of day-
care centers for children of pre-school age. Another example relates to the loss of
leisure time and the desire for leisure time products to be more convenient. Such
desire, tied to the technological developments surrounding VCR's, created a whole
new industry and lifestyle change for many.

There are many other trends or possible trends that may have an impact on the buying habits and tendencies of Americans in the coming decade. Such things as population shifts to different regions, continuing problems in the economy, environmental concerns, new governmental regulations, and the increasing rate of technological innovations may very well have major impact on the changing face of this society.

1. Factors that will influence market trends in the 90's

   a. Demographic trends, e.g., _____

   b. _____

   c. _____

   d. _____

2. Specific recent trends noted: Consequences:

   a. _____   a. _____

   b. _____   b. _____

   c. _____   c. _____

   d. _____   d. _____

3. Other trends to watch:

   a. _____

   b. _____

   c. _____

   d. _____

   e. _____

LISTING & COMPARING TRENDS

In small teams, discuss one of the following issues. Use the charts on page 83 to summarize your ideas.

1. What are some of the major trends in various countries outside the U.S.? Which trends exist in more than one country? (List both the trend and the countries involved). What do you think the implications of those trends will be for new products or services in this decade?
2. What are some of the major trends in one particular country? How are those trends either similar to or different from those listed above? What do you think the implications of those trends will be for new products or services in this decade?

1. TREND   COUNTRIES   IMPLICATIONS

a. _____   _____   _____

b. _____   _____   _____

c. _____   _____   _____

d. _____   _____   _____

e. _____   _____   _____

2. Trend in _____   COMPARISON
         (country)

a. _____   _____

b. _____   _____

c. _____   _____

d. _____   _____

e. _____   _____

FINAL TEAM TASK

In small teams, do the following:

1. Choose someone to lead your meeting.
2. Choose one or more trends noted previously, either internationally, or in a specific country or region, and then predict and discuss what new (or greatly expanded) products or services will come as a result of the trends. If you want, you may choose to focus on how the trends will lead to products in one particular industry OR in various industries.
3. Focus on the following:
   a. Predicting new products or services in the next 10 years (and next 20-30 years) from the trends.
   b. Thinking of as many possible new products or services from one or related trends.
   c. Discussing the implications of the trends and the new products on business or on people's lives.
4. When the team concludes the above work, representatives should prepare visual aids for the team's presentation to the larger group.

REPORT ON TRENDS/NEW PRODUCTS

Write a clear and concise report summarizing your thoughts on the final team task. This report should clearly indicate the trends being discussed, their implications for new products and services, and what effects the new products and services will have for individuals, companies, and so on.

Segment 8

Building a Better Mousetrap

from *20/20*, 11/13/86
Runtime: 13:45
Begin: 1:01:43

Previewing

KEY QUESTIONS

1. How do people come up with new ideas?
2. How do companies come up with new products and innovations?
3. What new product can you create?
4. How will you present your new product proposal to top management?

DISCUSSION

1. How do you personally come up with new ideas? _____

_____

   a. Describe the process you go through and talk about when and where you
     tend to get new ideas, e.g., in the car on the way to work. _____

_____

   b. What generally happens before you have the new ideas, e.g., a deep
     discussion with others? _____

_____

   c. What do you generally do after you have a new idea, e.g., write them
     down for the future, talk with friends? _____

_____

2. How do companies generally come up with new products or innovations?

_____

_____

3. Look at the shape below, or choose another shape, and then come up
   (with others) as many different ideas of what the shape could be.

1. _____   6. _____
2. _____   7. _____
3. _____   8. _____
4. _____   9. _____
5. _____   10. _____

PREDICTION

Building a better mousetrap is a common expression in English, which relates
to any improvement on an established product or service, not just traps for
catching mice. Based on what you now know of the title of this segment,
what information do you think will be included in the video segment?

1 _____

2 _____

3 _____

4 _____

GLOBAL VIEWING

GETTING THE GENERAL IDEA

View the whole segment, taking notes as you desire. Use the following questions to guide your listening. Then compare and discuss your notes with others to check your comprehension.

1:01:43-
1:12:02

1. Who? _____

_____

_____

2. What? _____

_____

_____

3. Where? _____

_____

_____

4. Why? _____

_____

_____

5. How? _____

_____

_____

6. Examples: _____

_____

_____

_____

EXECUTIVE SUMMARY

Write a clear, concise and quick one-page executive summary of the main ideas and important details and examples. After you have finished, e.g., after 15 minutes, exchange your executive summary with someone else. Read the other person's summary, adding any important points that are missing. Read for meaning only, do NOT correct the other person's language. Repeat as necessary.

INTENSIVE VIEWING

NOTETAKING FOR DETAILS

1:01:43-
1:12:02

View the video again and fill in the notetaking grid below:

1. Person who first said "Genius is 1% inspiration and 99% perspiration.":

   _____

2. Show where products are displayed: _____

3. Place where the show is held annually: _____

4. Size of the industry (in dollars): _____

5. Daily fee of consultant Roger von Oech: _____

6. Type of consulting Roger von Oech does: _____

7. Popular creativity technique: _____

8. Meaning of "Synectics": _____

9. George Prince' words about ideas: _____

10. One example of new product due to Synectics: _____

11. Any other example of such a product: _____

12. The first thing a Synectics facilitator asks a company executive to do:

    _____

13. Key word used to stimulate new thoughts: _____

14. View in brainstorming toward wild ideas: _____

15. Type of thinking taught in school: _____

16. Problem with the 'mowbot': _____

17. Four stages of the creative process, according to Mr. von Oech:

    1. _____

    2. _____

    3. _____

    4. _____

PREPARING QUESTIONS TO ASK

Compare your notes with others to check your comprehension. Then, together, prepare a list of questions to ask other comprehension consultants or to watch for in the video.

1. _____
2. _____
3. _____
4. _____
5. _____

Language Focus

VOCABULARY CHECK

1:01:43-
1:12:02

Read the sentences below to see how the *italicized* words are used. Watch the video again, listening for the sentences below. Then use the *italicized* word in another sentence.

1. Almost every product here is going to be *obsolete* in the next few years, and people have to be creative in order to come up with new products to keep their edge. _____

   _____

2. Some companies have their own staff of clever engineers and designers who get paid to *churn out* marketable new ideas. _____

   _____

3. Creativity often requires a willingness to explore *unconventional* paths, i.e., to move away from the traditional. _____

   _____

4. George Prince says that ideas don't just happen, you have to go wandering around in your mind for the material to *make connections*.

   _____

   _____

5. A Gillette employee said "We spent some time...*visualizing* ourselves as a piece of hair and getting shampooed and what kinds of reactions we felt."

   _____

   _____

6. Although they allowed us to sit in with them, they asked that certain material *be kept confidential.* _____

_____

7. His objective in the meeting was to be a *facilitator* of the discussion, not to give orders to everyone. _____

_____

8. The group was invited on an excursion, a mental journey to *stimulate* new thought processes. _____

_____

9. It's good to stimulate the *daydreaming* part of your mind because that's where your creative thinking is done. _____

_____

10. The creative person adopts four different hats in the course of first generating and then *implementing* new ideas. _____

_____

11. Is this idea right for the market now? Is the *timing* right? _____

_____

Postviewing

BRAINSTORMING

Brainstorming involves getting people together to create as many ideas, including wild ideas, as possible so people can break old habits of thinking and come up with new ways of solving problems. In small teams, do the following:

1. Pick any product category you desire, such as cars or computers or stereo equipment.
2. Choose someone on the team to write down the ideas.
3. Brainstorm to come up with as many new features or innovations in your product category as you can. You may wish for anything you desire. Remember these guidelines:
   a. Encourage many ideas, wild ideas, ideas which add to or combine other ideas, funny ideas, etc.
   b. Actively listen to each other. Active listening here can loosen you up for creative thinking of your own.

c. Keep the pace fast.
d. Don't criticize ideas now. The first stage is to come up with as many ideas as possible. Later on, you will have time to analyze and critique ideas.

4. Report the results of your brainstorming to the larger group.
5. Keep your written ideas for the final task.

RELATED READING: PRODUCT DEVELOPMENT

The article on pages 93 and 94 appeared in *The Economist*. It is an excellent description and analysis of new product development in Japan. Your task is to:

1. Read the comprehension and discussion questions below to guide your reading.
2. Read the article quickly for main ideas and important points. Ignore words you do not understand.
3. Discuss your answers to the questions with others.
4. Report your summary and commentary to the class or write an executive summary and commentary.

COMPREHENSION QUESTIONS

1. What has been the traditional reputation of Japanese companies regarding innovation? _____

_____

2. Why is this reputation false for Japanese companies in Japan?

_____

3. What is product covering? _____

_____

4. What is product churning? _____

_____

5. What is parallel development? _____

_____

6. What are the speed and cost ratios of Japanese vs. western firms in product development?

   a. Speed: Japanese ____ : ____ Western
   b. Cost: Japanese ____ : ____ Western

7. What three factors account for these speed ratios?

   a. _____

   b. _____

   c. _____

8. Why haven't Japanese manufacturers been able to transfer all these practices abroad? _____

   _____

9. Generally speaking, how are Japanese consumers different from consumers elsewhere? _____

   _____

DISCUSSION QUESTIONS

10. What have you learned from this article? _____

    _____

11. Do you think this rapid pace of innovation will increase, continue as is, or slow down in the 21st century? Explain your reasons. _____

    _____

12 Based on what you know of companies known for rapid new product development, what are the advantages and disadvantages of working for them?

    Advantages   Disadvantages

    a. _____   _____

    b. _____   _____

    c. _____   _____

What makes Yoshio invent

Western companies are supposed to be the masters of innovation, marketing and incisive management. Japanese firms have a reputation for borrowing ideas from abroad, making painstaking improvements and then, when everything is ready, churning out better-quality products in huge volumes at low prices. This reputation may still be partly true for Japanese companies abroad. At home, almost the opposite is the case, as many American and European companies trying to compete have been shocked to discover.

Foreign firms entering the Japanese market with a four-year technical lead have seen their products quickly matched—not copied, mind, but matched—and then left behind. Once Japanese manufacturers relied on slick production techniques to make them into awesome competitors. Today their most effective weapon is rapid innovation.

Take Sony's best-selling CCD-TR55, a miniaturised video camera and recorder ("camcorder") that weighs a mere 790 grams (1.5 lbs). To make the product palm-sized, Sony had to shrink 2,200 components into a space one-quarter the size they occupy in a conventional camcorder. Yet only six months after introducing the CCD-TR55 in June 1989, Sony had competition. Matsushita, followed by its stablemate, JVC, launched even lighter look-alikes. Within a year, Sanyo, Canon, Ricoh and Hitachi were selling palm-sized camcorders as well.

The process of rushing out instant imitations is known in Japan as product covering. Rival manufacturers rush to produce their own versions just in case the pioneer's should prove to be a best-seller. With a target to aim at, the coverers know that the innovation is at least technically feasible. Reverse engineering—taking the product apart to see how it works—provides short-cuts. The top priority of companies is to prevent distributors and retailers from deserting their own camp.

Product covering is really just a part of an even more formidable Japanese process known as product churning. When developing a new product, western firms use a "rifle" approach, testing the market constantly and revising the product each time until it exactly meets the customer's needs before launching it. Japanese manufacturers, by contrast, tend to use a "shotgun" approach. For instance, around 1,000 new soft drinks appear annually in Japan, though 99% of them vanish within a year. New-product ideas are not tested through market research, but by selling the first production batch.

Kevin Jones, a consultant in McKinsey's Tokyo office, points out that nobody could imagine why people would want a hi-fi with not one, but two compact-disc players. The doubters included Sharp, the firm that launched the machine. Nevertheless teenagers bought the machines to mix tracks from separate CDs onto tape. Within months both Sanyo and JVC followed with their own twin-CD machines.

Firms also engage in parallel development—developing second-and-third generation products along with the initial version. As soon as the pack catches up, the original innovator has a replacement for its own hit product ready to go. Only weeks after Matsushita launched a rival to Sony's palm-sized camcorder, Sony hit back with two new models-one even lighter, the other with yet more technical ⟩

features. Companies that fail to ride each successive wave of innovation risk being washed away. This looks wasteful. But according to a study by McKinsey, Japanese companies develop new products in a third to half the time spent by their western counterparts, at a quarter to a tenth of the cost. Three factors help Japanese pull off this feat:

- **Japan's army of engineers**. Japanese companies are reaping the benefits of the country's enormous investment in education, especially in engineering schools. Technical literacy is now more widely diffused throughout Japanese business than anywhere else in the industrial world. Japan has 5,000 technical workers for 1m people. The comparable figure for America is 3,500, for western Germany 2,500; no other country comes close.

- **Catalogue design**. Instead of designing every component of a new product from scratch, Japanese engineers reach instinctively for the parts catalogue. By using off-the-shelf components wherever possible, they devote their most creative engineering skills to fashioning a product that is 90% as good as a product designed from scratch might be—but only half the price of a completely original version.

- **Free flow of information**. Unlike western firms, which tend to hand their suppliers the skimpiest of specifications when seeking a price quotation for a new component, Japanese manufacturers share their most secret plans, send their top staff to help out and hand over any proprietary know-how needed. They then leave the supplier to get on with the job of developing the part needed for the new product. With so much trust and exchange of staff, says McKinsey's Mr. Jones, product-development information can flow between a company and its suppliers while a new product is still only a gleam in an engineer's eye. The lack of job-hopping among Japanese engineers limits the leakage of information to competitors.

Even Japanese firms have not been able to transfer all these practices abroad. Flooding the market with new products, even imitations, is important in Japan because firms are determined not to lose access to scarce, and often rigid, dealer and distribution networks. Abroad, this matters less. Tarnishing their reputation with a poor product is also less of a concern because many new versions are aimed at a small core of sophisticated customers who will try anything new. The extraordinary appetite of all Japanese consumers for new gizmos can also make an ageing product-line fatal to a firm's prospects, as many failed camera manufacturers discovered in the 1980s.

Abroad, new products still have to be chosen and developed more carefully. A single dud can damage a carefully nurtured image. And falling a small step behind is not so threatening once brand loyalty has been established. Nevertheless, the new-product treadmill Japanese companies face at home has already given them an enviable prowess in foreign markets. Moreover, any western firm hoping to grab a chunk of the huge Japanese market will have little choice but to step on to the new-product treadmill too.

FINAL TEAM TASK: NEW PRODUCT PROPOSAL

In the same small teams you were in for the brainstorming session, do the following:

1. Choose someone to lead your meeting(s).
2. Select the top two new product (or service) ideas from your earlier brainstorming that you think have the most potential to be successful (OR, if you wish, the new products which would be the most creative).
3. Discuss and decide on the following matters. This will make up most of your product proposal.
   a.   What features make the product unique?
   b.   What impact would it have on society or on its buyers?
   c.   What target markets is it intended for?
   d.   How would you position it?
   e.   What price do you propose for it at first? Why? How does this compare with existing products?
   f.   What brand name would you use for it?
   g.   How would you package it?
   h.   Where will it be sold?
   i.   How do you propose to promote it, e.g. advertising, in-store displays, etc.? Be specific.
   j.   Any other relevant, important information.
4. Prepare visual aids, e.g., poster drawings, scale models, overhead transparencies for your presentation to the larger group.
5. Present your new product proposal to the CEO and other managers. You will have 15 minutes to present and 5 minutes to answer any questions from the audience. Every team member should have an active role in the presentation.
6. Listen actively to the other new product proposal presentations, take notes (for a final memo) and ask questions. You may use the grid below to help in your notetaking:

Product: _____

Features: _____

Impact: _____

Target market: _____

Positioning: _____

Price: _____

Brand name: _____

Packaging: _____

Place (distribution): _____

Promotion: _____

FOLLOW-UP EXECUTIVE SUMMARY

After listening to the other product proposal(s), summarize the key points of one presentation (not your own). Then give your own recommendation on whether the new product should be a "GO" or "NO GO."

Segment 9

A 30 Second Spot

from *20/20*, 3/25/88
Runtime: 14:44
Begin: 1:12:06

Preview

KEY QUESTIONS

1. What kind of advertising appeals to you? What kind does not appeal to you?
2. How much influence does advertising have on your decision to buy one product rather than a competing product?
3. What factors must be considered when advertising a new product? When advertising a product overseas?
4. How would you advertise the products developed in segment 8?

DISCUSSION

1. What are your favorite advertisements and TV commercials? _____

   _____

   Why do you like them? _____

   _____

2. How much influence do you think that advertising has over people's decisions to buy products? _____

   a. What other factors influence people to buy or not buy a product or to buy one product rather than another? _____

      _____

   b. Which of these factors do you think is most important to most people?

      _____

   c. Which of these factors is most important to you? Why?_____

      _____

PREDICTION

Based on the title of this segment, *A 30 Second Spot,* what information do you think will be included in this video segment?

1. _____
2. _____
3. _____
4. _____

GLOBAL VIEWING

NOTETAKING

1:12:06-
1:19:23

As you watch the first part of the video, focus on global comprehension, not specific details. You may use the space below to take notes (main ideas only).

_____

_____

_____

_____

_____

_____

_____

_____

_____

_____

_____

_____

_____

_____

_____

_____

_____

THE 30-SECOND SUMMARY

In small teams, discuss and decide on the main ideas of the segment. Then have a representative give a 30-second report to the audience.

Intensive Viewing
NOTETAKING FOR IMPORTANT POINTS

Skim the grid below and then view the video again and fill in the grid:

1:12:06-
1:19:23

1. Three things TV commercials should do:

   grab   _hold_   _sell_

2. The key information about the advertising people: _small + open_

   Focus: topical   _irreverent_

3. The key information about the client: _TV personality_

4. The key question for the advertisers: _How wld you sell the product._

5. The premise for the product: _take advantage th. she is well-known_

6. The advertising strategy: _a little bit more spec. + expensive + glamorous_

7. The advertising style: _Topical + irrelevent, tongue-in-cheek sell the sizzle of the product, not the nitty-gritty_

THE 60-SECOND SUMMARY

In small teams, compare notes for understanding. Then have a representative give a 60-second report to the audience.

CONCERNS ABOUT THE COMMERCIAL

As you view the next part of this segment, focus on the issues below. Fill in the missing information as you view the video.

1:19:23-
1:26:50

1. The client's views: _____

2. The advertising people's views: _____

3. The second version of the commercial: _____

4. The main differences between the two versions: _____

5. The commercial finally chosen: _____

6. The reporters' views about the two commercials: _____

Language Focus:

FORMAL AND INFORMAL LANGUAGE

Informal language is frequently used in business, especially among colleagues and people we know fairly well. Using language informally (for our purposes here) includes using:

1. run-on sentences connected by "and" (see example below)
2. phrases instead of sentences: ("How about that deal?" for "That was a good deal, wasn't it?")
3. using informal variations of standard words: ("yeah" for "yes")
4. using well-known substitutes for standard words: ("uh-huh" for "yes" and "UN-uh" for "no")
5. fillers and hesitation devices: ("like," "you know") These are more common among teenagers and younger people. The devices are useful to recognize, but they represent sloppy language use, so be careful about using them.

1:16:41-
1:18:12

Listen again to the short video excerpt for informal language. Next, underline examples in the transcript below. Then in small groups, change the discussion from informal to more standard business English. Finally, present your new, standard English discussion to the audience.

EXAMPLE:

Mr. K: <u>Marisa, why don't you—why don't we do something—We'll all think of ways to go and then you write them and I'll put them on the wall.</u>

Standard Business English

Mr. K: Let's think of ways to go Marisa, why don't you write them, and I'll put them on the wall.

DISCUSSION:

Mr. K: Why don't we just do the glamour aspect of it, you know—

Mr. B: Glamorous chicken.

Mr. K: Glamorous chicken, glamorous chicken.

Mr. B: Yeah.

Mr. K: How about playing off the name, "Chicken by George"? Maybe we could do famous Georges. How about the Chairman of the Board idea.

Mr. B: That's interesting.

Mr. K: Yeah, let's go with the hostess aspect. How about the fact that's it's a designer chicken?

Brown: The point of this discussion is to get those first off-the-wall expressions on the wall, decide which are unnecessary—

Mr. K: Take it down. Take it down.

Brown: ...and then try to develop the rest into scenarios.

Mr. K: Everybody liked the hostess thing first. Well, let's just do executions off of that.

Mr. B: I got it. It's like Phyllis George comes up with this new chicken and thought she'd try it out on a few of her friends.

Mr. K: It's a very good idea.

Mr. B: Really understated.

Mr. K: All the limousines could be coming up—

Mr. B: All the limousines could be coming up and then they show Joe Namath in it (a famous American sports hero), you know.

Mr. K: Right. Joe ordered this, Don ordered this. And it's always like famous people turning around. Then you see the reveals of the people turning around like Joe, Don, buh, buh, buh, buh, buh—

Mr. B: Right, right.

Mr. K: The line for this could be just plain, "If it's good enough for them, it's good enough for you."

Mr. B: Uh-huh.

Mr. K: You know, just as a—You know—

Mr. B: That's good. That's great.

Mr. K: Like, you know, if it's good enough for them—

Mr. B: That's the truth.

Mr. K: Like, it's good enough for you, like—

Mr. B: That's great, because Miss Minimum who wants a piece of the glamour.

Mr. K: Right, that's great.

Mr. B: That's it. I love it.

Brown: [*voice over*] Not for long. Faster than you can say "trust me," that idea died on the table.

Postviewing

READING FOR INSIGHTS

Read the excerpts from the following article by Kaori Shoji for two purposes:
(1) to learn more about cultural differences that make an impact on
advertising in other countries, and (2) to learn more about important
factors to consider in advertising. Then fill in the grid below. This
information may help you in your final task.

Do NOT stop and look up words you do not know. Focus on general
understanding.

Differences between American and Japanese Cultures

    1. _____

    2. _____

Differences between American and Japanese Advertising

    1. _____

    2. _____

    3. _____

    4. _____

Key Factors in Advertising (overseas)

    1. _____

    2. _____

    3. _____

Custom-Made Campaigns
Set aside those Madison Avenue mores and tailor advertisements to suit the taste
of Japanese consumers

"Forget about what was good back home. More than likely, it won't apply to
Japan." That is the blunt advice Yoshiko Koike, executive creative director of
J. Walter Thompson Japan, offers foreigners who want to advertise in Japan. A
20-year veteran of the ad wars, Koike points to a campaign she helped prepare for
South African raw-diamond supplier De Beers. "It took me 10 years to convince
them that Japanese women don't smile and kiss their husbands when they receive
diamonds as gifts," she says. "Instead they shed a few crocodile tears and pretend
they're angry at their husbands for spending so much money."

Before taking Koike's advice, De Beers ran ads in Japan depicting Western couples in evening dress. "The ads," she recalls, "reflected the standard Western mentality that equates diamonds with grandeur." But J. Walter Thompson's 1988 Christmas campaign broke new ground by showing a tired salaryman and his hard-working-wife in their tiny apartment. Upon receiving the sparkling present, she snaps at her extravagant spouse, "Oh, you stupid!" The ads was well received and De Beers quickly scored a marketing success, which coincided with the growth in popularity of diamonds in Japan. When De Beers first entered the market, Japan constituted a mere 1% of world diamond sales. The country now accounts for 32% of all diamonds sold.

Koike...is continually astounded by the number of foreign firms that stumble when it comes to creating a positive image in Japan. Like other commercial ventures, the business of advertising can be a series of never-ending trials. But the results are far from disheartening. Some of Japan's liveliest and most-memorable advertisements are produced when American companies customize their message to the special requirements of the Japanese market.

"The Japanese place undisputed trust in the printed word and television," says Yukichi Amano, noted columnist of "CM-Watching," a daily advertisement-critique column in the Asahi Shimbun. "So advertising success equals marketing success, more so than in any other country in the world." A selection of the most conspicuous foreign ad campaigns...offers some valuable lessons for companies attempting to plug their products in Japan.

One American company that appears to understand the Japanese market is Coca-Cola (Japan) Co. Since the firm was established in 1957, its ads have targeted Japan's idealized notion of the American lifestyle. "Coca-Cola ads embody the Japanese love for the all-American way of life," says company spokesman Hideaki Nawa. "That love is something that has never changed over the years."

Coke's universal message is "Drink Coke and feel good." In Japan feeling good has evolved into an obsession, says Ko Sakata, chief creative officer of McCann-Erickson Hakuhodo, who has worked on the Coke account for the past 23 years. The 1987 "I feel Coke" campaign "hit a nerve," explains C. Patrick Garner, director and senior vice president of Coca-Cola Japan. The TV commercials showed happy young Japanese enjoying the good life, Coke cans prominently in hand, at barbecues, picnics and Christmas parties, and viewers were surprised at how Americanized they appeared. "If the Japanese can hold a Coke can and look good," says Garner, "that means it has become as established as green tea." With a 93% share of the cola beverage market, Coke has become the most powerful American brand in Japan, according to the 1990 Landor Associates Image Power survey.

Procter & Gamble Far East's Pampers is another example of a superior marketing campaign. P & G introduced their disposable diapers to Japan in 1977, creating an immediate sensation. Market share climbed to 90%, but plummeted to 5% in the space of six years as domestic competitors such as Uni-Charm moved in with cheaper, better-quality diapers that were supported by well-defined ad campaigns.

For a while, it looked like another riches-to-rags story in Japan, but P&G rallied by developing an improved version of Pampers and creating a coherent sales message to go with it. In 1985 Grey Daiko Advertising, Inc., one of the first U.S.-Japan advertising joint ventures with more than $740 million in billings, launched the Talking Diaper campaign. Director of creative services Tateo Ikunaga's concept is simple. It's the delivery that's different—a talking diaper that soothingly persuades baby, mom and hopefully the viewer, that Pampers is the only disposable diaper that fits perfectly into this loving relationship....

"The ad isn't bold or unique," says Michiko Shimamori, editor-in-chief of the trade monthly Kokoku Hihyo (Advertisement Critique). "But the message delivered is so sincere that it wins trust right away." P & G currently has a 30% market share.

While these ads for American products are seemingly commonplace, a powerful element of advertising success in Japan is the weird, bizarre, suggestive. Consider these recent campaigns:

- Blue whales float across the sky in a Suntory beer commercial.
- A close-up of Christopher Lloyd (of *Taxi* and *Back to the Future* fame) saying "TV, TV-er, TV-est!" promotes Fuji Television.
- Two giant beetles lock tentacles in a Japan Railways poster.
- An old man caresses the bare foot of a sexy teen in an Americaya Shoe Store campaign.
- A shot of panties stretched across rows of female buttocks advertises Wacoal lingerie.

Taboo is fair game in Japan. "What may be inconceivable to us can be the most natural thing for the Japanese," says J. Mitchell Reed, CEO of Grey Daiko Advertising. Though not the sole reason for Wacoal's success, its daring, sexually explicit (and some might say sexist) ads have helped the company secure a healthy 34% share of the lingerie market.

Permanence of image is clearly more important than breaking social conventions. As Shigesato Itoi, the nation's most famous copywriter, puts it, "A good ad is one that hits you, and lodges in the brain." Impact is especially important because the life span of a Japanese ad is extremely short. Posters stay up from three weeks to two months as opposed to a minimum of six months in the United States. Television campaigns have slightly longer lives, but even the most popular individual ads rarely run longer than six months. This rapid-fire arrangement allows agencies to drop losers quickly and expand on winners.

This can frustrate American executives, who often stick with an ad campaign regardless of initial performance in the hopes that it will increase brand awareness. Koike of J. Walter Thompson says, "It's the quarterly reporting obligations that prevent them from taking the long-term view. If they would only invest their time and funds in a series of good campaigns, the results could be surprising."

If there is a key to advertising success, perhaps it is "Keep an open mind," says Dai-Ichi Kikaku's Etsuko Yoneyama. "Japanese advertising is so full of the unexpected." Apparently, agencies have trouble selling foreign managers on the value of surprise.

Reprinted with permission by **Business Tokyo**, March, 1991, pp. 12 & 16.

ANALYZING COMMERCIALS & ADS

Watch and analyze three or more TV commercials, using the following grid to guide your analysis. First watch a commercial on TV and then fill in the grid. Continue until you have completed the work. Do the same with magazine ads. When you finish, compare your grid with others, finding similarities and differences.

COMMERCIALS	1	2	3	4
Product	_____	_____	_____	_____
Brand	_____	_____	_____	_____
Featured features	_____	_____	_____	_____
Type of appeal, e.g., direct, humorous, mysterious, etc.	_____	_____	_____	_____
Type of people	_____	_____	_____	_____
Type of places	_____	_____	_____	_____
Type of situations	_____	_____	_____	_____
Action words used	_____	_____	_____	_____
	_____	_____	_____	_____
	_____	_____	_____	_____
Positive words used	_____	_____	_____	_____
	_____	_____	_____	_____
	_____	_____	_____	_____
	_____	_____	_____	_____
Negative words used	_____	_____	_____	_____
	_____	_____	_____	_____
Unique feature of the commercial	_____	_____	_____	_____

FINAL TEAM TASK

In small teams, do the following:

1. Choose someone to lead your team.
2. a. Select one of the products that were proposed at the end of segment eight, *Building a Better Mousetrap,* and prepare an ad campaign for that product. The ad campaign should include both a TV commercial and a magazine ad.
   b. OR select any product you desire and prepare the ad campaign.
3. Choose the country in which you want you ads to appear.
4. Choose the target market segments for the product.
5. Brainstorm to get as many ideas as you can.
6. Once you have enough ideas, narrow down your selections to the best options.
7. Come up with scenarios for the themes.
8. Choose the best theme.
9. Write up the scenario and any dialogue or passage for the commercial and ad in a team report.
10. Practice the commercial.
11. Prepare the magazine ad for display. Also decide on what kind, and if possible, the specific magazines in which you would place the ad.
12. Present your commercial to the audience (your class, OR videotape your commercial for airing on TV).

For both #11 and #12, be sure to indicate the country and market segments for which you designed your ad campaign.

ADVERTISING CRITIQUE

After listening to and reading the other advertising campaigns, choose one and then write up a 1-2 page critique on both the TV commercial and the magazine ad. Evaluate the campaign on the following criteria plus any others that may be relevant. Be sure to explain your opinions with reasons for each question below.

1. How well does it grab the viewer's/reader's attention at first?
2. How well does it hold the viewer's/reader's attention?
3. What is the main message of the campaign?
4. Is that message made clear?
5. How effective is the appeal used to sell the product to that particular audience (country and market segment)?
6. Could the same approach be used to sell the product in your country/segment? Why or why not?
7. Would you buy this product? Why or why not?

Segment 10

Competition in Europe in the 1990's and Beyond

from *Business World*, 7/14/91
Runtime: 3:49
Begin: 1:38:01

Note: This segment actually begins at 1:26:53 and has a runtime of 15:57, but only the last section is used.

Previewing

KEY QUESTIONS

1. What are the most important political, societal, and economic events and changes in the world at the present time?
2. How are those events changing, and how will they change the international business environment?
3. What actions, if any, should national governments take to support, subsidize or protect key business sectors?
4. What are the trends for business in different industries in different areas of the world in the 1990's and beyond?

DISCUSSION

In small groups, discuss the following questions:

1. What are the most important events and changes in the world today that may affect the business environment? Use the chart below.

	International	Domestic
Political		
Economic		
Societal		
Technological		

UNIT 4 GLOBALIZING FOR THE FUTURE

2. How are these events changing, or how will they change, the business environment?

a. Political: _____

_____

b. Economic: _____

_____

c. Societal: _____

_____

d. Technological: _____

_____

3. What actions should national governments take in supporting, subsidizing or protecting key business sectors? Why? _____

_____

_____

_____

_____

PREDICTION

Based on the title of the segment, *Competition in Europe in the 1990's and Beyond*, and your own knowledge of Europe after 1992, what information do you think will be included in the video segment?

1. _____

2. _____

3. _____

ESSENTIAL WORDS TO KNOW

The words below are used in the video segment. Familiarize yourself with the meaning of the words before you view the tape. First, a general definition is given. Then, in the space that follows, write a sentence with the italicized word(s) included.

1. *free trade* = trade internationally that is characterized by an absence of governmental or other restrictions

_____

_____

2. *import quotas* = limits that a national government puts on foreign goods that may come into the nation

_____

_____

3. *investment* = the putting of money and other resources into something with the idea of that profits will eventually be earned

_____

_____

4. *national champion* = a company or industry that is considered to be one of the best the nation has to offer and which may be given support by the national government

_____

_____

5. *subsidies* = support that a government gives to its people, its companies, and so on.

_____

_____

Global Viewing

DEBATE PREPARATION

Form debate teams of two to four people per team. At some point after viewing the video (and after having done some outside research), you will debate the following issue:

Governments should subsidize corporations and protect them from foreign competition.

As you view the video, watch for the contrasting views on this issue. Write notes in the chart below.

1:38:01-
1:42:50

PRO	CON

PREPARING QUESTIONS

Based on what you know you do not understand from the video, prepare questions in your teams to listen for in the second viewing.

1. _____
2. _____
3. _____
4. _____
5. _____

ANSWERING YOUR QUESTIONS

1:38:01-
1:42:50

As you view the segment again, answer your questions, and those of others. Then compare your notes with those of other students to check your comprehension.

1. _____
2. _____
3. _____
4. _____
5. _____

Intensive Viewing

NOTETAKING

1:38:01-
1:42:50

The notetaking form below has been partially filled in with key words that are mentioned in the segment. Before you view the segment again, complete the form below with what you already know from your first two viewings. Then as you view it again, complete the form. After you finish, compare your notes with others to check your comprehension.

1. International trade problem: _____
2. Nissan: _____
3. Import quotas: _____
4. Importance of summit: _____
5. American auto manufacturers: _____
6. Ford: _____
7. GM: _____
8. Germany: _____
9. European auto market: _____

10. Surplus: _____

11. Beliefs in Great Britain: _____

12. Beliefs in France: _____

13. Groupe Bull: _____

14. R & D: _____

15. French policy: _____

16. Concerns over American products: _____

17. Airbus: _____

Language Focus

WORD ASSOCIATION

Match the words in the first column with their meanings in the second column.

___ 1. reasonable

___ 2. economic invasion

___ 3. transplant

___ 4. subsidies

___ 5. clearly

___ 6. (good) bottom line

___ 7. contribution

___ 8. booming

___ 9. in essence

a. handouts; capital injection

b. improvement to one's industry

c. profits

d. soaring; doing well

e. market battle in new territory

f. basically

g. foreign factory in country

h. obviously

i. nonthreatening

DISCUSSION STRATEGIES FOR EXPRESSING DISAGREEMENT

Several people in this segment use specific expressions that signal that a different view from what has been said. Read the examples below. Then, with a partner, take turns criticizing some business or government/business policy and responding to that criticism.

1. *I want to be very clear on this point.*

Jacques Lebhar, CFO, Groupe Bull: "*I want to be very clear on this point.* There's no government subsidies to Bull. Various government supports to our R & D programs are under review by the European Community. As for the rest, the government decided the capital injection...is normal in business life in particular.

Criticism: _____

_____

Response: _____

_____

2. *The (British) argue...*

Sander Vanour, Business World: "*The British argue* that one man's capital injection is another man's subsidy and views the French policy of supporting so-called national champions as outmoded."

Criticism: _____

_____

Response: _____

_____

3. *If you...and you are only..., but you are not..., then you are not...*

Timothy Sainsbury, U.K. Minister of Trade: "*If [you]* set out to be the national champion *and you are only* the national champion as far as the States or Britain is concerned, *but you're not* fit to compete in the worldwide competition, *then you're not* a very good national champion."

Criticism: _____

_____

Response: _____

_____

4. *But ...*

Sander Vanocur (to report someone else's view of Japanese investments
   in the U.K): "*But* the chairman of French automaker Peugeot claims
   England is being used as an aircraft carrier to launch an economic
   invasion."

Criticism: _____

_____

Response: _____

_____

5. *That's nonsense.*

Ian Gibson, CEO, Nissan, U.K.: "*That's nonsense.* We're as European as
   any of the Europeans in essence, nowadays, and in global terms, we're
   in exactly the same situation as Ford in Europe or G.M. in Europe.

Criticism: _____

_____

Response: _____

_____

Post Viewing

Read the following article to help prepare for your final tasks. Read for
general understanding, answering the questions that follow.

Europe after 1992

A unified Europe will provide a formidable global economic challenge

The formation of a borderless, tariff-free common market within the European
Community will be largely complete at the end of 1992. The resultant economic
restructuring will create pan-European companies that will be very competitive in
the global market, says Daniel Burstein, author of Euroquake.

As the European Community unites and allows citizens of one country to pass
freely throughout all other member countries, it will also surpass the United States
as the largest single economic market in the world, according to Burstein. The
European Currency Unit (ECU) will become the currency for all of the
Community by 1997, backed by a "EuroFed" central bank with the participation
of the major national banks.

December 31, 1992, marks the deadline set eight years before for the official integration of a single European market and the free movement of EC citizens among all member countries. This represents only the first major step to total European unity, Burstein notes. Other integrative steps will include creating a common European currency, common foreign and defense policies, and eventually a formal political union.

The 1992 deadline will not be met completely, but it has served a purpose in galvanizing efforts to create the Community, according to Burstein. The efforts have encountered severely turbulent political battles and upheavals, such as the reunification of Germany and the inclusion of two more countries—Spain and Portugal—in recent years. Burstein predicts that, while progress is being made, EC proponents may encounter even more hazards along the way to unification, including pressure from an independent-leaning Britain, unequal economic growth patterns among member nations, and increased and aggressive competition from outside forces, such as Japanese and some American corporations.

A reunited Germany, now the largest and richest country in the Community, will play an increasingly powerful role in the new European Community, as it continues to rebuild former East Germany and begins to help develop other countries in Eastern Europe, according to Burstein. The reunification of Germany in 1989-1990 caused many to speculate on the doom of the Community because of Germany's lopsided power position and its traditional ties to the east. This has not proved to be a problem, because almost all Germans feel themselves firmly ensconced in the revitalized EC.

American companies will feel the strain from the increased global competition from European firms, especially in the manufacturing sectors, the author says. While firms in Europe and Japan are restructuring and developing their capital, American firms are hampered by a large trade deficit and balance-of-payments problems caused by the governmental budget deficit. Burstein expects American service-sector companies to do well in the new European market, but manufacturing and many high-tech industries may suffer. He also predicts a much more severe recession in the United States than the one in 1991 that will last from 1992-1993 until 1997, while Japan and Europe will continue to expand their economies.

*Reprinted with permission from The Futurist, September-October, 1991.Published by The World Future Society. Copyright © 1991. All Rights Reserved.Source: *Euroquake: Europe's Explosive Economic Challenge Will Change the World* by Daniel Burstein. Simon & Schuster, 1991.

1. What is happening in Europe? _____

_____

2. What are some of the specific steps being taken to make this happen?

_____

_____

_____

3. What are some of the problems being faced as this happens?

_____

_____

4. What will Germany's role in this be? _____

_____

5. How will all of this affect American companies? _____

_____

6. What is the prediction for the U.S.A. between 1992-1997?

_____

THE THREE-WAY BATTLE

Read the article on the next page and then fill out the grid following it. This may also help you in the debate.

Where The Three-Way Skirmishes Are Hottest in Europe

TOTAL SALES IN EUROPE

Level of Japanese Competition
- ● Serious
- ● Moderate
- ○ Worth watching but still low

Autos $120 BILLION ●

Nissan, Toyota, Honda are building manufacturing bases in Britain. As national quotas fall, they hope to use these plants to raise overall Japanese market share from current 12% to 17% in 1998. GM, Ford are spending big to boost productivity, while Europeans seek alliances to compete. Potential shakeout victims: Fiat, Renault.

Communications $77 BILLION
○ Networks ● Cellular

As national barriers fall in 1992, Alcatel, Ericsson, Siemens are likely to face pressure from AT&T, Northern Telecom, Motorola, and each other in network gear. Japanese firms NEC, Panasonic, Mitsubishi are moving in on Motorola in the booming $3 billion mobile phone market.

Computers $44.3 BILLION ●

American companies led by IBM, Compaq, Hewlett-Packard hold big edge. And Fujitsu, Hitachi, Toshiba are moving in through acquisitions, direct sales, and making deals with Europeans. Weakened by recession and lagging technologies, Groupe Bull, Philips, Olivetti heighten European worries of further Japanese takeovers.

● **Consumer Electronics $40 BILLION**

With the Japanese in control of the camcorder and VCR market, high-definition TV will mark the future for European leaders Thomson, Grundig, and Nokia. Boost may come if EC sets favorable HDTV standards. But Sony, Toshiba, and Panasonic have set up local factories and are poised for growth.

● **Tires $31 BILLION**

Sumitomo and Bridgestone have 7% market share each after purchase of Dunlop and Firestone. Michelin is still No. 1, with a third of the market, but its attempts to fight off Bridgestone have hurt the whole industry. Pirelli wants merger with Continental to rival Michelin, Bridgestone, and Goodyear.

Office Equipment
● Copiers/$15 BILLION
● Printers/$11 BILLION

Canon/Olivetti joint venture and Minolta have chopped market share of low-end copiers from Rank Xerox. Canon, Konica target high-speed models. Hewlett-Packard rules laser and ink-jet printers but Canon, Kyocera, Germany's Mannesman-Tally are coming on strong.

Machine Tools $17.8 BILLION ○

Germany, Italy, Switzerland are still world leaders. But Japan's Amada pushes in metal working tools, and Yamazaki Mazak, with local producers, moves into numerically controlled machines and lathes. Midsize Europeans such as Gildmeister, Trumpf, Maha are winning in customizing standard tools.

Construction Equipment

$15 BILLION ○

Ever since EC-imposed anti-dumping duties in 1985, Komatsu and other Japanese rivals have been producing locally or in joint ventures. Japanese market share for crawler-excavators doubled by 1990, at 32%. Caterpillar still leads, but Japanese have edge in technology, design.

● **Semiconductors $10.7 BILLION**

The Europeans' 38% share of their own market is being eroded by unprecedented buildup of Japanese capacity in memory chips, while Americans stay strong in microprocessors. Philips, Siemens, SGS-Thomsoncan't match massive technology spending by Japan's NEC, Hitachi, and U.S.'s Intel, Motorola.

*Reprinted from June 3, 1991 issue of Business Week by special permission, copyright © 1991 by McGraw-Hill, Inc.

According to the article, who led in 1991 in each industry mentioned and who do you think will lead by the year 2000? Put a check (✔) on the line under the market you think will lead. Then compare and discuss your responses with others.

Industry	1991-Europe/U.S.A./Japan			2000-Europe/U.S.A./Japan		
Autos	—	—	—	—	—	—
Communications	—	—	—	—	—	—
Computers	—	—	—	—	—	—
Consumer Electronics	—	—	—	—	—	—
Tires	—	—	—	—	—	—
Office Equipment	—	—	—	—	—	—
Machine Tools	—	—	—	—	—	—
Construction Equipment	—	—	—	—	—	—
Semiconductors	—	—	—	—	—	—

PAIR DEBATING FOR FLUENCY

In pairs, debate one or more of the following questions. One person should argue for and the other should argue against each question. If there is a third person involved, that person can be the person in the middle, with a position that "it depends." The spaces below are for your reasons. If you have time, think of the best reasons on the other side of the question; e.g., if you believe the "for" position, think of arguments for the "against" position and vice versa.

In order to develop your speaking fluency, try debating one person for 8 minutes; then change opponents and debate with the second person for 6 minutes; finally, change opponents again and debate the third person for 4 minutes.

1. Should businesses pay more money to domestic suppliers to support their own nation's economy? Why or why not?

   FOR   AGAINST

   _____   _____

   _____   _____

   _____   _____

2. Businesses should be able to build factories anywhere in the world and to move production to other countries whenever they want.

   FOR   AGAINST

   _____   _____

   _____   _____

   _____   _____

3. Governments should limit the assets that foreign corporations can own in the countries.

   FOR   AGAINST

   _____   _____

   _____   _____

   _____   _____

FINAL TEAM TASK: SEMI-FORMAL DEBATING

The issue to be debated is as follows:

Governments should subsidize corporations and protect them from foreign competition.

After your instructor gives you instructions on the specific format of the debate, meet in your debating teams, and do the following:

1. Prepare your best arguments in writing both *for* and *against* the statement above. The reason for doing both is twofold:

   a. to deepen your own understanding of the issue, and
   b. to help you to prepare a better debating plan and strategy.

2. Decide who will do what in the debate; i.e., who will present your side's position, who will defend it, who will attack the other side's position and who will conclude your team's debate.

3. Prepare your communication strategy for dealing with different matters that may come up during the debate.

4. Practice debating. Some teammates should simulate your opposing team. This will help you to speak more effectively in the time permitted, to become familiar with your strategy and basic ideas, to see if your argument has any weak points that could be corrected before the debate, and for any other feedback that might be helpful. Practice only with your teammates.

5. Remember these important pointers:

   a. Keep focused on your role. For example, if you are supposed to defend your team's position from the opponent's attack, do not launch another, different attack at the opponent. Stick to the issues raised by your team and attacked by your opponent.

   b. Listen well to what the other team says. If you planned carefully, you will probably not hear any surprises, but always listen intently, just in case.

   c. Adjust your message, when necessary, when the other team surprises you with content or communication strategy.

   d. State 3-5 solid reasons for your position and then support that position with relevant statistics, details, examples, or anecdotes. Do not simply keep repeating one point.

6. Debate as instructed. When watching the other debates, evaluate each debater using the following questions as criteria:

   Content
   - How well is the talk organized?
   - How well developed is the content?
   - How logical is the content?

   Communication (both verbal and non-verbal)
   - How interesting is the speaker to listen to and watch?
   - How persuasive is the speaker?
   - How comfortable does the speaker appear?

7. After each debate, vote to see which team won. Then discuss both the strengths of each speaker AND suggestions for each speaker for future communication efforts.

EXECUTIVE SUMMARY

1. Write a clear and concise report which summarizes the main issue, then summarizes the best reasoning both for and against the issue, and finally concludes with your own recommendation and reasons; OR

2. Write a short report discussing the trends in one industry in the world in the 1990's and your recommendation for one corporation in that industry.

Segment 11

Golden Arches in Red Square

from *PrimeTime Live*, 1/25/90
Runtime: 7:13
Begin: 1:42:53

Previewing

KEY QUESTIONS

1. How have eating habits and food preferences in your country changed in the last 50 years? How are your eating habits and food preferences different from your parents? From your children?
2. What could a restaurant chain from overseas do to become successful in your national or local market?
3. What skills are important in negotiating internationally?
4. How good are you in these important skills?

PREDICTION

Get into teams to think up and write down as many questions as you can that you think might be answered when you watch the segment later.

USEFUL WORDS TO KNOW

The words below are used in the video segment. Familiarize yourself with the meaning of the words before you view the tape. First, a general definition is given. Then, in the space that follows, write a sentence with the italicized word(s) included.

1. *gear up* = prepare for

_____

2. *exceptional* = extremely good, outstanding

_____

3. *persistence* = continuing effort in spite of problems

_____

4. *shortages* = situations where the supply cannot meet the demand
   for goods or services

_____

5. *turn out to be* = become

_____

6. *turn out* = produce

_____

7. *take (something) for granted* = view something as common and not
   appreciate

_____

8. *upwardly mobile* = moving up the ladder of success

_____

Global Viewing

ANSWERING YOUR QUESTIONS

1:42:53-
1:50:06

View the video segment, *Golden Arches in Red Square*, for general understanding. As you watch, note down your answers to the questions your team thought up in the prediction exercise.

QUESTIONING EACH OTHER

Compare your answers with those of your teammates. Then ask other teams your questions and answer theirs.

CULTURE COMPARISON

1:42:53-
1:50:06

View the video segment again. As you watch, note down any differences between what you see and hear in the video and what you would see and hear in your own culture.

RUSSIAN CULTURE   YOUR CULTURE

_____   _____

_____   _____

_____   _____

_____   _____

COMPARING NOTES

Compare and discuss your impressions with others to check your comprehension and to deepen your understanding of cultural similarities and differences around the world.

Intensive Viewing

LISTENING FOR DETAILS

Skim the notetaking form below. Then view the videotape one more time, filling in the form as you go. When you finish, compare your notes with others to check your comprehension.

1:42:53–
1:50:06

1. Name of famous cathedral: _____

2. Time of year: _____

3. Number of seats inside McDonald's: _____

4. Number of seats outside: _____

5. Number of customers predicted per day: _____

6. Letter of English alphabet not found in Russian: _____

7. George Cohon's prediction of Soviet reaction: _____
_____

8. Dollar amount of investment in the restaurant: _____
_____

9. Time it took to negotiate the deal: _____

10. Problem in negotiation: _____
_____

11. Problems with Soviet beef: _____
_____

12. Problems with Soviet potatoes: _____
_____

13. Square footage of farm plant: _____

14. Source country for the apples: _____

15. Weekly production of hamburger buns: _____

16. Diane Sawyer's reaction to the french fry: _____
_____

17. Number of jobs required in restaurant: _____

18. Number of people who applied: _____

19. Hourly wage of workers: _____

20. Wage and incentives are more than a _____ makes.

21. The skill some Muscovites may find shocking: _____

22. Cost of a Big Mac equals the cost of _____ elsewhere.

23. Soviets now have an appetite for _____, as reflected by the popularity of shops like Estee Lauder and Christian Dior.

24. George Cohon's plan for McDonald's in Russia: _____

    _____

25. The shape of the sundae is similar to that of the _____

26. Profit division: Soviets: ____%; McDonald's of Canada: ____%

27. The hitch (problem) with profits: _____

Language Focus

WORD ASSOCIATION

Match the words in the first column with those in the second column that are similar in meaning or relate to each other in a general way.

1. incentives ____	a. quick, active
2. shortages ____	b. practice
3. desperate ____	c. multi-lingual
4. hitch ____	d. benefits
5. rare ____	e. unfamiliar
6. gear up ____	f. struggling
7. dynamic ____	g. lack of supplies
8. well-educated ____	h. problem

Write sentences with the following words:

1. incentives: _____

2. shortages: _____

3. hitch: _____

4. gear up: _____

5. dynamic: _____

Postviewing

UPDATE AFTER ABOUT 1.5 YEARS

Read the information below and then answer the questions that follow.

Moscow-McDonald's, located on Pushkin Square, just off Tverskaya Street, is a rubles-only restaurant. It was conceived to serve the Soviet people and they have enthusiastically embraced the restaurant as their own. The restaurant opened with a crew of 630, making it the largest McDonald's crew in the world. Since opening day the crew has almost doubled to more than 1,100 people. In total, more than 1,500 Soviets are employed by McDonald's at the restaurant, its office, and McComplex, the Food Production and Distribution Centre for McDonald's in Moscow.

- McComplex, located in the Moscow suburb of Solntsevo, supplies Moscow-McDonald's with locally source food products. The centre provides a strictly controlled, state-of-the-art food processing environment, in accordance with McDonald's rigid specifications and standards. More than 40 quality control checks are conducted on beef products alone.

- Moscow-McDonald's works actively with local agricultural suppliers to improve the quality of products, increase yields, and introduce new agricultural methods.

- Moscow-McDonald's restaurant in Pushkin Square continues to be the busiest McDonald's restaurant in the world. In just 20 months of operation, the first McDonald's restaurant in Moscow has served 22 million Muscovites and guests of the city, averaging between 40,000 and 50,000 customers per day.

Vladimir Malyshkov, Chairman of Moscow-McDonald's, said people continue to visit Moscow-McDonald's in record numbers. "Our customers wait in line anywhere from 20 minutes to 90 minutes, but once they get inside the restaurant, they get their orders filled in less than 60 seconds," he said. "And they still get a smile and an invitation to come back again.

"Moscow-McDonald's has also become a place where Muscovites and visitors come to enjoy themselves," said Mr. Malyshkov. "More than providing food and service, our customers have come to view McDonald's as a special place where they can meet their old friends and make new ones," he added.

- On a monthly basis, the restaurant has been serving approximately: 476,667 Coca-Cola/ Fanta/Sprite drinks
- 486,667 orders of french fries
- 390,000 milkshakes
- 330,000 Big Mac sandwiches
- 326,333 sundaes
- 226,667 apple pies

"Giving back to the community" is a basic corporate philosophy at McDonald's and this commitment has grown with the worldwide expansion of the Company. Today, McDonald's is active in youth programs and fundraising activities in all 54 countries in which it operates.

*Reprinted with permission from McDonald's Restaurants of Canada Limited.

QUESTIONS

1. Can you use international currency at the Moscow-McDonald's? ____

2. From the fact sheet above and from a prediction made in the video, what are two indicators that the business has been a success so far?

   _____

   _____

3. From the fact sheet on page 125 and the video, what are some indicators that McDonald's presence has helped the Russians?

   _____

   _____

4. How many customers does Moscow-McDonald's average per month?

   _____

SPECIAL RESEARCH ASSIGNMENT

Go to (or call) the McDonald's (or other fast food) restaurant nearest you and do the following:

1. Note down the prices for each item below:

   Coca-Cola: _____ (also Fanta/Sprite)

   french fries: _____

   milkshake: _____

   Big Mac: _____

   sundae: _____

   apple pie: _____

2. Note down the other items on the menu not listed in the simplified menu above:

_____

_____

_____

_____

3. Observe how long people have to wait before they enter the restaurant.
   How long? _____

4. Observe how long people have to wait on average once they are in the restaurant until the time they get their orders.
   How long? _____

5. Observe how friendly the McDonald's employees are to the customers.
   Are they friendly? _____

6. At the prices found in your local McDonald's restaurant and the numbers of orders and customers per month found at Moscow-McDonald's, calculate the average amount that each Soviet customer would spend if he or she went to your local McDonald's.

   _____

DISCUSSION

Compare and discuss your findings in small teams. Then report your team's conclusions to the audience.

Read the following excerpts from *Big Mac** by Peter Fuchs about Den Fujita of McDonald's in Japan. Then discuss the questions with others in your team.

Big Mac

...[Den] Fujita is the multimillionaire entrepreneur who in the past 20 years has made McDonald's one of the most successful American companies in Japan.

...Since opening his first store in 1971, Fujita has built McDonald's Co. (Japan) Ltd. into the dominant player in the country's $4 billion burger market. Last year his 750 outlets rang up sales of $1.3 billion, and he predicts that by the year 2000 sales will reach $3.7 billion.

In a land in which success is achieved by adapting products and services to fit Japanese tastes, Fujita has achieved fame as a marketing maverick for his insistence on changing nothing. Granted, McDonald's stores in Japan aren't exactly the same: the menus are written in Japanese, the customers and staff are mostly Japanese, and a few items, like the Teriyaki burger, corn soup, and ice coffee may be unfamiliar to McDonald's customers outside Japan. But in almost every other way, from the uncomfortable plastic chairs to the quality of the service to the smell of the french fries, a McDonald's in Japan looks, feels and tastes like any McDonald's restaurant in Iowa, Denmark or Argentina.

"McDonald's has been extraordinarily successful, and has clearly dominated its competition," says an American marketing consultant in Tokyo. "Its success can be attributed in part to its ability to maintain very high quality standards and secure good locations. The bottom line: I eat there quite a lot."

...For his part, Fujita sees himself as an agent of cultural change. He wants to make his countrymen think, look and act differently, and he doesn't plan to topple the government or reform the schools to do it. He just wants to modify the way they eat.

...Fujita owes his success to two strategic decisions he made. One was to keep the McDonald's system intact, adhering religiously to its massively detailed manual, which prescribes every facet of the operation from the height of its buns to the temperature of its soft drinks. "Ray Kroc invented an unbeatable system," Fujita says. "I knew from the start that adapting this system to fit Japanese culture would be a disaster. I realized that my job was to change the culture instead.

The other maneuver was to put his first outlet in the heart of Tokyo's fashionable Ginza district. Kroc urged him to aim at the suburbs, following the strategy that was the key to McDonald's success in America. But Fujita was adamant and convinced the directors at Mitsukoshi, one of the Ginza's most exclusive department stores, to lease him the space.

"Kroc's concept of quality, service, cleanliness and value didn't exist in Japan before we arrived," Fujita says. "Before 1971, there wasn't even a restaurant industry as such. Yet once we introduced McDonald's, we got away from the mom–and–pop scale operation to companies with tens of thousands of employees. The more firms like us, the better for the Japanese consumer."

McDonald's first diversification move in Japan, a joint venture with retailing giant Toys "R" Us, will also benefit the consumer, according to Fujita. "There's a lot of synergy between their stores and ours," he says, "and we are planning to build several large shopping malls together. We are working with the government to amend the law that limits the construction of large retail outlets. If we succeed in developing our first project, I think it will create opportunities for other U.S. firms to follow."

*Reprinted courtesy of **Business Tokyo,** 104 Fifth Avenue, New York, NY, March 1991, pp.12 &16.

QUESTIONS

1. How much does the average McDonald's outlet in Japan sell per month?_____ per day? _____

2. What are the keys to McDonald's success in Japan?

   _____

   _____

3. In your opinion, how did Fujita's strategic decisions help him to succeed?

   _____

   _____

4. In your opinion, what are the similarities between McDonald's and Toys "R" Us that make mutual agreements worthwhile?

   _____

   _____

5. "Fujita sees himself as an agent of cultural change." How do other products, e.g.,VCR's and camcorders, change cultures?

   _____

   _____

6 What dangers, if any, are there in such changes to traditional cultures?

   _____

   _____

7. How should global companies respond to critics of such changes?

   _____

   _____

RATE YOURSELF AS A NEGOTIATOR

Read the following passage and rate yourself as a negotiator. Then discuss the various skills needed by negotiators in your country and internationally.

...Some people do not become good negotiators until they rethink their approach. This scale is based on personal characteristics necessary to successful negotiation. It can help you to decide the potential you already possess and also identify areas where improvement is needed. Circle the number that best reflects where you fall on the scale. The higher the number the more the characteristic describes you. When you have finished, total the numbers circled in the spaces provided.

I am sensitive to the needs of others.	10 9 8 7 6 5 4 3 2 1
I will compromise to solve problems when necessary.	10 9 8 7 6 5 4 3 2 1
I am committed to a win/win philosophy.	10 9 8 7 6 5 4 3 2 1
I have a high tolerance for conflict.	10 9 8 7 6 5 4 3 2 1
I am willing to research and analyze issues fully.	10 9 8 7 6 5 4 3 2 1
Patience is one of my strong points.	10 9 8 7 6 5 4 3 2 1
My tolerance for stress is high.	10 9 8 7 6 5 4 3 2 1
I am a good listener.	10 9 8 7 6 5 4 3 2 1
Personal attack and ridicule do not bother me unduly.	10 9 8 7 6 5 4 3 2 1
I can identify bottom line issues quickly.	10 9 8 7 6 5 4 3 2 1

TOTAL   _____

If you scored 80 or above, you have the characteristics of a good negotiator. You recognize what negotiating requires and seem willing to apply yourself accordingly. If you scored between 60 and 79, you should do well as a negotiator but have some characteristics that need further development.

If your evaluation is below 60, you should go over the items again carefully. You may have been hard on yourself, or you may have identified some key areas on which to concentrate as you negotiate.

*Reprinted with permission by Crisp Publications Inc. from *Successful Negotiation* by Robert B. Maddux, pp.22-23. All rights reserved.

FINAL TEAM TASK: NORTH-SOUTH NEGOTIATIONS

Form small negotiating teams of 2-3 persons. Half the teams will be from one of the highly industrialized countries (North Team), and the other half will be from countries in the process of industrializing (South Team). In your team, do the following:

1. Study the role instructions for your side. Do NOT read the role instructions for the other side. If you do, it will be announced on the *ABC News ESL Video Library: Focus on Business* TV broadcast to you and all your counterparts and may result in your counterparts toughening their negotiating position.
2. Prepare your team's position and your team and individual strategies and tactics for the upcoming negotiation. If you have time to spare, practice your strategies and tactics with each other.
3. Meet and conduct negotiations with your counterparts from the other country.
4. After the negotiations have concluded, hold a mutual press conference with visual aids to announce the results of the negotiations.

You do NOT have to come to an agreement with the other side. Only come to an agreement if you are comfortable that the deal will serve your side's interest.

NORTH TEAM

- You represent McDonald's or another restaurant chain from Australia, Canada, Germany, Japan or the U.S. Your company is very interested in expanding operations through a joint venture abroad, similar to and yet better for your company than what McDonald's has done in the Soviet Union.

- In your negotiations, be sure to focus on the following:
    a. ability to control the other side's people
    b. ability to coordinate plans
    c. currency risks and restrictions to the business
    d. political risks to the business (coups, freezing of assets, etc.)
    e. problems with different accounting and information systems
    f. differences in corporate cultures
    g. maintaining high quality goods and services
    h. getting the best locations for the new restaurants
    i. freedom to expand as much as you want without government restrictions
    j. waiver of all taxes to the government for the first 10 years

- Your preference is to control at least 75% of the business and to be able to transfer profits out of the country without restriction. You realize that you may have to compromise on some issues, but you want to achieve as good a deal as possible so that your own careers within the company continue to improve.

SOUTH TEAM

- You represent the government of a developing country which would like to bring in the sophisticated operating systems and technology in agricultural development and food processing that have made McDonald's and other fast food restaurant chains so successful around the world. You have heard of McDonald's success in the Soviet Union and look favorably on the deal that the Soviets made with McDonald's Restaurants of Canada, Limited.

- In your negotiations, be sure to focus on the following:

  a. ability to control the other side's people

  b. ability to coordinate plans

  c. their assistance in training your country's people in advanced agricultural production and food processing

  d. their ongoing contributions to various charities or government programs

  e. problems with different accounting and information systems

  f. differences in corporate / government cultures

  g. control over locations of new restaurants

  h. control over how much the new restaurant chain expands

  i. other: _____

- Your preference is to control at least 75% of the business and to able to keep all profits within the country. However, you realize that that may not be possible and you may have to compromise on some issues. Still, you want to achieve as good a deal as possible so that your country benefits and so that your own careers within the government continue to improve.

FINAL TASK: NEGOTIATION SUMMARY REPORT

Write a clear and concise report, including the following items:

1. What the decision was and whether there was agreement.
2. If there was agreement, list everything agreed to in the negotiations.
3. If there were points of disagreement, explain the stumbling blocks (problems) that need to be overcome.
4. If there was no agreement, and the negotiations ended in failure, explain what happened to cause the failure.
5. Your assessment of the other team's negotiating strategies and tactics.

Segment 12

Mergers & Acquisitions: Back to Basics

from *Business World, 12/23/90*
Runtime: 6:55
Begin: 1:50:10

Previewing

KEY QUESTIONS

1. What are the advantages and disadvantages of companies merging with or acquiring other companies?
2. What are some of the dangers of companies acquiring other companies overseas?
3. What are some of the cultural differences in negotiation styles and characteristics?
4. What factors should be taken into account when setting up to negotiate and make a deal to acquire, merge, or form a strategic alliance with another company overseas?

CATEGORIZING SKILLS & TRAITS IN NEGOTIATION

Negotiators absolutely need certain kinds of skills and characteristics. Other skills and characteristics, while useful, are not absolutely essential. On page 134, there are 41 words that could be used to describe a negotiator. Categorize and rank 30 of these skills and characteristics. If you do not know what a word means, focus on the words you do know.

1. analytical
2. angry
3. arrogant
4. aware of other's position
5. calm
6. competitive
7. confident
8. considerate
9. cooperative
10. courteous
11. creative
12. diplomatic
13. direct
14. disciplined
15. dogmatic
16. efficient
17. empathetic
18. ethical
19. experienced
20. fair
21. firm
22. flexible
23. formal
24. goal-oriented
25. honest
26. hostile
27. humorous
28. idealistic
29. indirect
30. informal
31. logical
32. naive
33. openminded
34. patient
35. perceptive
36. persistent
37. realistic
38. sarcastic
39. sensitive
40. serious
41. tolerant of conflict

ESSENTIAL	USEFUL	NOT USEFUL
1. _____	_____	_____
2. _____	_____	_____
3. _____	_____	_____
4. _____	_____	_____
5. _____	_____	_____
6. _____	_____	_____
7. _____	_____	_____
8. _____	_____	_____
9. _____	_____	_____
10. _____	_____	_____

DISCUSSION

In small teams, discuss the following questions:

1. What are the advantages and disadvantages of merging with or acquiring another company?

Advantages	Disadvantages
1. _____	_____
2. _____	_____
3. _____	_____
4. _____	_____
5. _____	_____

2. What are some of the dangers involved in acquiring companies overseas?

_____

_____

_____

3. What should a company look for when deciding IF and WHEN to acquire another company? _____

_____

_____

ESSENTIAL WORDS TO KNOW

The words below are used in the video segment. Familiarize yourself with the meanings of the words before you view the tape. First, a general definition is given. Then, in the space that follows, write a sentence with the *italicized* word(s) included.

1. *acquisition* = the situation in which one company buys another

_____

2. *asset stripping* = the situation in which a company sells off parts of another company it has acquired, typically to make quick profits

_____

3. *corporate raider* = a businessperson who buys stock in companies and then tries to take control of the company or sell his/her stock quickly at a large profit

_____

4. *financial engineering* = the financial strategies a company uses to maneuver, buy, and make money on another company

_____

5. *hostile bid* = an offer to buy another company against the second company's management's wishes. This typically leads to a takeover battle

_____

6. *junk bonds* = bonds that can be purchased for ten cents on the dollar (or 10%) of their actual value and that corporate raiders and other "financial engineers" use to buy large companies. Since the buyers usually only have a small amount of the money needed to make the buys, the value of the bonds often depends on whether the buyers can strip the assets of the new company. Junk bonds were very popular on Wall Street in the 1980's

_____

7. *leveraged buy-out (LBO)* = the purchase of a company, typically using junk bonds, with only a small amount of equity capital and large loans and debts

_____

8. *merger* = the situation in which two companies combine to become one

_____

9. *takeover battle* = the situation in which one company tries to acquire another company which, in turn, fights to remain independent

_____

ASKING QUESTIONS

This segment is entitled *Mergers and Acquisitions: Back to Basics*. In teams, think up and write down as many questions as you can that you think will be answered in the segment.

1. _____

2. _____

3. _____

4. _____

5. _____

Global Viewing

ANSWERING YOUR QUESTIONS

1:50:10-
1:57:05

View the video segment for general understanding. As you watch, note down any answers to questions your team thought up. Then compare your understanding with your teammates. Then ask other teams your previous questions and answer the questions that the other teams ask of you.

1. _____

2. _____

3. _____

4. _____

5. _____

NEWS SUMMARY

1:50:10-
1:57:05

View the whole segment again, taking notes as you go. Use the following questions to guide your understanding. Compare notes with others to check your comprehension when you finish.

Who? _____

_____

What? _____

_____

When? _____

_____

Where? _____

_____

Why? _____

_____

How? _____

_____

Examples: _____

_____

_____

Intensive Viewing

NOTETAKING

1:50:10-
1:57:05

Look at the notetaking form below. Then view the videotape one more time, filling in the form as you go. Compare your notes to others to check your comprehension when you finish.

1. The big news since Friday: _____

2. What Carl Icahn wants Pan Am to do: _____

3. AT&T's action: _____

4. The new wave: _____

5. Results of Georgia Pacific's action: _____

6. Cost of the action: _____

7. What T. Marshall Hahn, Jr. calls the move: _____
_____

8. Philip Morris' action: _____

9. Cost of Matsuhita's action: _____

10. Cost of AT&T's attempted action: _____

11. Philip Keevil's definition of strategic merger: _____
_____

12. Reason for AT&T's action: _____

13. Number of junk bond offerings in 1989: _____

14. Number of junk bond offerings in 1990: _____

15. What the junk bond band has done: _____

16. What Irwin Jacobs says is happening: _____
_____

17. How this compares to the 1980's: _____

18. What's happening with mega-deals: _____

19. Who the corporate buyers of the 90's will be: _____
_____

20. Cash on hand in 1979 of the five companies mentioned: _____

21. Cash on hand in 1990 of the five companies mentioned: _____

22. The trend in the types of corporate buyers: _____

23. Where the future merger activity is: (1) _____
(2) _____ (3) _____ (4) _____

24. The area that is undercapitalized: _____

25. Condition of Drexel: _____

26. Trend and % in global merger activity: _____ by _____%

27. Trend and % in domestic merger activity: _____ by ____%

28. When LBO's do well: _____

29. When LBO's don't do well: _____

30. Reason to worry about the situation: _____

31. What could happen to Apple Computer: _____

32. By what companies: _____

_____

LISTENING CLOZE

View the first part of the video again and fill in the blanks below.

Announcer: From ABC News, this is Business World, with Sander Vanocur and Stephen Aug. Now from New York, here's Sander Vanocur.

1:50:21-1:51:37

Sander Vanocur: In news _____ Friday's closing bell, there's a lot of talk this _____ about a possible Pan Am-TWA merger. But Pan Am's chairman, Thomas Plaskett, _____ to be challenging TWA to put it money where its _____ are. He wants a virtually unconditional bridge loan to keep Pan Am flying. TWA's Carl Icahn, on the _____ _____ , says he wants Pan Am to file for _____ first, so any money he lends will be better protected. The Pan Am-TWA talks come in the same week when the AT&T tender _____ for NCR was making headlines. Both, as business editor Stephen Aug reports, are part of a new wave of old-style mergers and acquisitions, companies merging for _____ reasons.

Stephen Aug: (voice over) Georgia Pacific Corporation is the largest forest products concern in the nation. The main reason: it won a _____ battle last spring, buying the rival, Great Northern Nekoosa, for $3.7 billion. At Georgia Pacific _____ in Atlanta, chief executive Marshall Hahn says the merger is working out _____ than expected, a good example of what's now being called a strategic _____.

T. Marshall Hahn: It was an old fashioned kind of combination. Not financial engineering. Not _____ stripping. But a strategic combination of two very strong _____ companies in an industry to create an even stronger company. I believe you will see _____ ____ that type of strategic acquisition.

Language Focus

WORD FORMS

The following words were used in the segment. Complete the grid below by adding the other forms of the given words:

NOUN	VERB	ADJECTIVE
1. _____	_____	financial
2. acquisition	_____	_____
3. merger	_____	(no adj. form)
4. access	_____	_____
5. _____	afford	_____
6. _____	_____	emphatic
7. _____	challenge	_____
8. _____	_____	capitalized
9. bankruptcy	go_____	_____
10. _____	_____	diversified

SYNONYMS & ANTONYMS

Match the words in the first column with those in the second column that are either general synonyms or antonyms. Then, to the left of the number, circle S for synonym or A for antonym. Finally, write a sentence with each word from the first column. Note that this exercise continues on page 141.

S / A 1. go out of business ____   a. buy with financial engineering

S / A 2. well-capitalized ____   b. weary

S / A 3. rival ____   c. target (v)

S / A 4. deep pockets ____   d. domestic

S / A 5. takeover ____   e. dissolve

140

S / A   6. global ____   f. cash rich
S / A   7. doing mega-deals ____   g. going back to business basics
S / A   8. strategic combination ____   h. competitor
S / A   9. shell shocked ____   i. capital shortage
S / A 10. go after (a company) ____   j. hostile bid

1. _____
2. _____
3. _____
4. _____
5. _____
6. _____
7. _____
8. _____
9. _____
10. _____

Post Viewing

SUMMARIZING NEGOTIATION STEPS

The following passage is from a book by Robert B. Maddux, entitled *Successful Negotiation*. Read it and then summarize the key points below.

Below is a brief summary of the six steps common to each negotiation. Keep these in mind before you engage in your next negotiation.

Step 1
I plan to get to know the party with whom I will be negotiating. My objective will be to keep initial interaction friendly, relaxed and businesslike.

Step 2
I expect to share my goals and objectives with the other party. At the same time I anticipate learning the goals and objectives of the other side. If possible, the atmosphere during this step will be one of cooperation and mutual trust.

Step 3
To start the process, specific issues will be raised. I plan to study all issues before the negotiations begin to identify where my advantages might lie insofar as splitting or combining issues is concerned. Once this has been done, the issues can be dealt with one by one.

Step 4

Once the issues have been defined it is essential to express areas of disagreement or conflict. Only when this has been done will it be possible to resolve the differences in a way that is acceptable to both parties.

Step 5

The key to any successful negotiation is when both parties reassess their positions and determine what level of compromise is acceptable. During this step I plan to remember the give-get principle (basically, you have to give something in order to get something).

Step 6

The final step is when both parties affirm any agreements that have been reached. I plan to ensure that there is no misunderstanding later by putting the agreements in writing (when applicable), and sending a copy to the other side. Mutual agreement is the ultimate objective of any negotiation.

KEY WORDS

Step 1: _____

Step 2: _____

Step 3: _____

Step 4: _____

Step 5: _____

Step 6: _____

CULTURAL TENDENCIES IN BUSINESS

Various writers have discussed cultural differences that complicate business relationships and negotiations. Below are some tendencies that have been noted for Americans and Japanese . Look at the tendencies and, from your background knowledge, where your own national tendencies would be on the spectrum. Circling a "10" indicates that your culture's tendency is very similar to the Japanese tendency, while circling "1" shows that your culture's tendency is very similar to the American tendency. If your cultural tendency is in the middle, or you are not sure where it falls, circle "5" or "6." When you finish, discuss your tendencies with others.

JAPANESE ◄----- 10 9 8 7 6 5 4 3 2 1 -----► AMERICAN		
Focus on group	10 9 8 7 6 5 4 3 2 1	Focus on individual
Focus on consensus	10 9 8 7 6 5 4 3 2 1	Focus on compromise
Formal	10 9 8 7 6 5 4 3 2 1	Informal
Passive speakers	10 9 8 7 6 5 4 3 2 1	Assertive speakers
Patient	10 9 8 7 6 5 4 3 2 1	Impatient
Quiet & reserved	10 9 8 7 6 5 4 3 2 1	Outgoing & talkative
Indirect	10 9 8 7 6 5 4 3 2 1	Direct & frank
"Yes" is for under-standing	10 9 8 7 6 5 4 3 2 1	"Yes" is for agreement
Saying nothing is preferred over "no"	10 9 8 7 6 5 4 3 2 1	Saying "no" is preferred over nothing
Status is respected	10 9 8 7 6 5 4 3 2 1	Status is downplayed
Focus on long-term	10 9 8 7 6 5 4 3 2 1	Focus on short-term

MAKING STRATEGIC ALLIANCES WORK

Read the passage below to prepare generally for the final team task. After each paragraph, write a sentence in your own words which summarizes the main idea of the paragraph.

1. In today's highly competitive world marketplace, strategic mergers and acquisitions make a lot of sense. The purchases of Columbia Studios and CBS Records by SONY helped to give the hardware company much more access to the software side of its business. Matsushita's purchase of MCA, which owns Universal Studios is another such move. In addition to M & A's, however, there lies the whole are of cooperation between competitors through joint ventures and other cooperative arrangements. Witness, for example, the cooperative arrangements between IBM and Apple Computer, two fiercely competitive giants in the personal computer industry, which see distinct advantages in joining forces to forge better futures for both.

Main Idea: _____

_____

_____

_____

2. As with M & A's, joint ventures carry with them many dangers. Strong differences in company cultures or top executive personalities can doom such alliances to failure. One company may contribute fairly while the other works only to its own advantage. In addition, whenever two companies are joined in some way, decision-making will typically slow down. In an age when speed is increasingly an essential part of business, such delays can be extremely frustrating. Then, too, each company legitimately has different priorities, and some of those priorities may be more important than the alliance. Alliances need time to mature so as to fully benefit both parties.

Main Idea: _____

_____

_____

_____

3. If strategic alliances are so dangerous, then why should top executives risk their careers and their company futures on cooperating with competitors? There are various reasons. First, there may be important new research being done by one company that may leave others lagging behind. In such a scenario, two or more smaller companies may need to join forces for combined R & D work. Second, one company may have expertise in a market where another has a new product that might do very well in it. A strategic alliance in that market may help both to prosper where, without the alliance, both might have suffered. Third, joint ventures can be useful ways to bypass government restriction. There are many other reasons as well: desire for increased profits, opportunities for more efficient production, acquisition of manufacturing skills, decrease of financial risk, increase of capital, and so on.

Main Idea: _____

_____

_____

_____

4. If a company is thinking about entering into an alliance with another company, what things does it need to consider? Among many other things, it is essential to study everything ahead of time. A S.W.O.T. analysis can help a lot in this regard. Planning is a key, from taking care of what seem to be minor details in the operation to communicating to various stakeholders in the process, e.g., consumers, suppliers, employees, community leaders, etc. Gaining some kind of consensus among the managers who will be connected with the process is another key. The partner one chooses is critical. Does it make sense over the long term or is it merely a tactic to get something for nothing. Joint ventures are like marriages in some respects. Sensitivity to the other's needs and patience in ironing out the problems is important as well.

Main Idea: _____

_____

_____

_____

FINAL TASK: NEGOTIATING A STRATEGIC ALLIANCE

Form negotiating teams of 2-3 persons. Half the teams will be from a Japanese industrial company with deep pockets and a desire to enter a new market. The other teams will be from a company from the U.S.A. which hopes to become better-capitalized in order to become more competitive in the market. In your teams, do the following:

1. Study the role instructions for your side. The instructions for the Japanese Team are on page 147, and the instructions for the American Team are on page 148. Do NOT read the role instructions for the other side. If you do, it will be announced on the *ABC News ESL Video Library Focus on Business TV* broadcast to you and all your counterparts. This may result in harsh government fines against your company and may result in your counterparts toughening their position substantially.
2. Prepare your team and individual strategies and tactics for the upcoming negotiation. If you have time to spare, practice your strategies and tactics with each other.
3. Meet and conduct negotiations with your counterparts from the other company.
4. After the negotiations have concluded, hold a mutual press conference, with visual aids, to announce the results of the negotiations.

You do NOT have to come to an agreement with the other side. Only come to an agreement if you are comfortable that the deal will serve your side's interest.

NEGOTIATION SUMMARY

Write a clear and concise report, including the following items:

1. The decision. Was there agreement?
2. If there was agreement, list everything agreed to in the negotiations.
3. If anything was not agreed upon, explain the stumbling blocks that need to be overcome.
4. If there was no agreement at all, and the negotiations ended in failure, explain what happened to cause the failure.
5. Your assessment of the other team's negotiating strategies, tactics, and communication styles.
6. What you have learned about negotiating or about communicating from this task.

JAPANESE TEAM

Your company is a well-established, cash-rich, industrial products company in a sunset (mature, low-growth) industry in Japan, but which has little real experience or market overseas. Consensus has been reached within your company that an acquisition of a company overseas would be a good opportunity to expand into a new industry and new markets. An American company has just approached your company about forming some sort of strategic alliance with them. Your task is to negotiate the acquisition of that company. In your negotiations, be sure to focus on the following:

1. Acquiring the company, not just participating in a joint venture or loose strategic alliance. You estimate the purchase price to be $700,000,000.

2. Getting access to the new technology and markets that the other company possesses.

3. Establishing control over the other company's operations, including quality control, accounting, information systems, etc.

4. Keeping the top executives of the American company so that operations continue smoothly.

5. Establishing a regular reporting system to ensure clear and complete communications between the two companies.

6. Any other concerns you have. If you cannot acquire the company, you should make as good a deal as possible so that you are in a position of control, not just partnership. You want to use this venture to prepare for greater overseas expansion in the near future.

SPECIAL NOTE: Try to use Japanese communication tendencies throughout the negotiations.

Your company is a relatively new company with a new, high technology product that promises to become very popular throughout the industrialized world. However, in order to produce and market the product on a wide scale, you need a partner to capitalize your big manufacturing and marketing push. You have learned that a well-established, cash-rich, industrial products company in a sunset (mature, low-growth) industry in Japan is interested in investing in a company such as yours. You have approached them and they have agreed to enter into talks with you. Your task is to come up with an agreement that will enable your company to succeed internationally without losing control of the company to the Japanese. You would like them to purchase a 15% stake in your company for about $150,000,000. You would also be willing to sell them exclusive distribution rights in Japan. In your negotiations, be sure to focus on the following:

1. Joining a strategic alliance with the Japanese company, NOT merging with or becoming acquired by it.

2. Maintaining control over and limiting their access to your new technology. Companies have been known to steal the secrets of another company and then abandon the partnerships. Be careful.

3. Maintaining control over your operations, such as information systems, accounting, and so forth. If you can get help in improving your quality control system without risking the loss of your technological secrets, that would be desirable. But can you do that?

4. Finding out what exactly the Japanese company expects for their investment and when they expect it. This will include how and how often reporting requirements are to be met.

5. Any other concerns you have. You may have to sell more of the company than you would prefer to get the capital you need, but you should make sure that you will still control the company in the end. You want this venture to help your company become an international presence in your industry.

SPECIAL NOTE: Try to maintain American communication tendencies throughout the negotiations.